David A. RoSooth.

2010.

"Rob Bell is a central figure for his generation and for the way that evangelicals are likely to do church in the next 20 years."
New York Times

"A prophetic voice."
Christianity Today

"He could be one of the most important 21st-century Christian leaders."
Time

"The next Billy Graham?"
Chicago Sun-Times

"Rob Bell is one of the hottest names in contemporary evangelical life."
Boston Globe

"It isn't easy to develop an imagination, a thoroughly biblical imagination, that takes in the comprehensive and eternal work of Christ in all people and all circumstances in love and for salvation. Rob Bell goes a long way in helping us acquire just such an imagination. *Love Wins* accomplishes this without a trace of soft sentimentality and without compromising an inch of evangelical conviction in its proclamation of the good news that is most truly for all."
EUGENE H. PETERSON, Professor Emeritus of Spiritual Theology, Regent College and author of *The Message* and *The Pastor*

"*Love Wins* is a bold, prophetic and poetic masterpiece. I don't know any writer who expresses the inexpressible love of God as powerfully and as beautifully as Rob Bell! Many will disagree with some of Rob's perspectives, but no one who seriously engages with this book will put it down unchanged. A 'must read' book!"

GREG BOYD, senior pastor at Woodland Hills Church and author of *The Myth of a Christian Nation*

"In *Love Wins*, Rob Bell tackles the old heaven-and-hell question and offers a courageous alternative answer. Thousands of readers will find freedom and hope and a new way of understanding the biblical story – from beginning to end."

BRIAN D. MCLAREN, author of *A New Kind of Christianity* and *Naked Spirituality*

"Bell takes concepts we think we know about Christianity and flips them into a new light, using hermeneutic judo to push for Christianity as a way of life that's constantly being reinvented and reimagined, not some empty husk of withered ritual."

The Tennessean

LOVE

WINS

ROB BELL

AT THE HEART OF LIFE'S BIG QUESTIONS

LOVE WINS

Collins

an imprint of HarperCollins*Publishers*
77–85 Fulham Palace Road
London W6 8JB

www.harpercollins.co.uk

10 9 8 7 6 5 4 3 2 1

First published in the USA in 2011 by HarperOne
This edition 2011

A catalogue record for this book is available from
the British Library.

ISBN: 978-0-00-742073-5

Designed by Level C

Printed and bound in Great Britain by Clays Ltd, St Ives plc

CONTENTS

PREFACE   **MILLIONS OF US**   vii

CHAPTER 1 **WHAT ABOUT THE FLAT TIRE?**   1

CHAPTER 2 **HERE IS THE NEW THERE**   21

CHAPTER 3 **HELL**   63

CHAPTER 4 **DOES GOD GET WHAT GOD WANTS?**   95

CHAPTER 5 **DYING TO LIVE**   121

CHAPTER 6 **THERE ARE ROCKS EVERYWHERE**   139

CHAPTER 7 **THE GOOD NEWS IS BETTER THAN THAT**   163

CHAPTER 8 **THE END IS HERE**   193

ACKNOWLEDGMENTS   199

FURTHER READING   201

MILLIONS OF US

To begin with,
a bit about this book.

First, I believe that Jesus's story is first and foremost
about the love of God for every single one of us. It
is a stunning, beautiful, expansive love, and it is for
everybody, everywhere.

That's the story.
"For God so loved the world . . ."
That's why Jesus came.
That's his message.
That's where the life is found.

There are a growing number of us who have become
acutely aware that Jesus's story has been hijacked by
a number of other stories, stories Jesus isn't interested
in telling, because they have nothing to do with what

he came to do. The plot has been lost, and it's time to reclaim it.

I've written this book for all those, everywhere, who have heard some version of the Jesus story that caused their pulse rate to rise, their stomach to churn, and their heart to utter those resolute words, "I would never be a part of that."

You are not alone.
There are millions of us.

This love compels us to question some of the dominant stories that are being told as the Jesus story. A staggering number of people have been taught that a select few Christians will spend forever in a peaceful, joyous place called heaven, while the rest of humanity spends forever in torment and punishment in hell with no chance for anything better. It's been clearly communicated to many that this belief is a central truth of the Christian faith and to reject it is, in essence, to reject Jesus. This is misguided and toxic and ultimately subverts the contagious spread of Jesus's message of love, peace, forgiveness, and joy that our world desperately needs to hear.

And so this book.

Second, I've written this book because the kind of faith
Jesus invites us into doesn't skirt the big questions about
topics like God and Jesus and salvation and judgment
and heaven and hell, but takes us deep into the heart of
them.

Many have these questions.
Christians,
people who aren't Christians,
people who *were* Christians,
but can't do it anymore because of questions about
these very topics,
people who think Christians are delusional and
profoundly misguided,
pastors, leaders, preachers—
these questions are everywhere.

Some communities don't permit open, honest inquiry
about the things that matter most. Lots of people
have voiced a concern, expressed a doubt, or raised a
question, only to be told by their family, church, friends,
or tribe: "We don't discuss those things here."

I believe the discussion itself is divine. Abraham does
his best to bargain with God, most of the book of Job
consists of arguments by Job and his friends about the
deepest questions of human suffering, God is practically
on trial in the poems of Lamentations, and Jesus

responds to almost every question he's asked with . . . a question.

"What do you think? How do you read it?"
he asks, again and again and again.

The ancient sages said the words of the sacred text were black letters on a white page—there's all that white space, waiting to be filled with our responses and discussions and debates and opinions and longings and desires and wisdom and insights. We read the words, and then enter into the discussion that has been going on for thousands of years across cultures and continents.

My hope is that this frees you. There is no question that Jesus cannot handle, no discussion too volatile, no issue too dangerous. At the same time, some issues aren't as big as people have made them. Much blood has been spilled in church splits, heresy trials, and raging debates over issues that are, in the end, not that essential. Sometimes what we are witnessing is simply a massive exercise in missing the point. Jesus frees us to call things what they are.

And then, last of all, please understand that nothing in this book hasn't been taught, suggested, or celebrated by many before me. I haven't come up with a radical new teaching that's any kind of departure from what's been said an untold number of times. That's the beauty of the historic, orthodox Christian faith. It's a deep, wide, diverse stream that's been flowing for thousands of years, carrying a staggering variety of voices, perspectives, and experiences.

If this book, then, does nothing more than introduce you to the ancient, ongoing discussion surrounding the resurrected Jesus in all its vibrant, diverse, messy, multivoiced complexity—well, I'd be thrilled.

LOVE WINS

CHAPTER 1

WHAT ABOUT THE FLAT TIRE?

Several years ago we had an art show at our church. I had been giving a series of teachings on peacemaking, and we invited artists to display their paintings, poems, and sculptures that reflected their understanding of what it means to be a peacemaker. One woman included in her work a quote from Mahatma Gandhi, which a number of people found quite compelling.

But not everyone.

Someone attached a piece of paper to it.
On the piece of paper was written: "Reality check: He's in hell."

Really?
Gandhi's in hell?
He is?
We have confirmation of this?

Somebody knows this?
Without a doubt?
And that somebody decided to take on the responsibility
of letting the rest of us know?

Of all the billions of people who have ever lived, will only
a select number "make it to a better place" and every
single other person suffer in torment and punishment
forever? Is this acceptable to God? Has God created
millions of people over tens of thousands of years who
are going to spend eternity in anguish? Can God do this,
or even allow this, and still claim to be a loving God?

Does God punish people for thousands of years with
infinite, eternal torment for things they did in their few
finite years of life?

This doesn't just raise disturbing questions about God; it
raises questions about the beliefs themselves.
Why them?
Why you?
Why me?
Why not him or her or them?

If there are only a select few who go to heaven, which is
more terrifying to fathom: the billions who burn forever
or the few who escape this fate? How does a person end
up being one of the few?
Chance?
Luck?

Random selection?
Being born in the right place, family, or country?
Having a youth pastor who "relates better to the kids"?
God choosing you instead of others?

What kind of faith is that?
Or, more important:
What kind of God is that?

And whenever people claim that one group is in, saved, accepted by God, forgiven, enlightened, redeemed—and everybody else isn't—why is it that those who make this claim are almost always part of the group that's "in"?

Have you ever heard people make claims about a select few being the chosen and then claim that they're not part of that group?

Several years ago I heard a woman tell about the funeral of her daughter's friend, a high-school student who was killed in a car accident. Her daughter was asked by a Christian if the young man who had died was a Christian. She said that he told people he was an atheist. This person then said to her, "So there's no hope then."

No hope?
Is that the Christian message?
"No hope"?
Is that what Jesus offers the world?

Grace as do does

Is this the sacred calling of Christians—to announce that there's no hope?

The death of this high-school student raises questions about what's called the "age of accountability." Some Christians believe that up to a certain age children aren't held accountable for what they believe or who they believe in, so if they die during those years, they go to be with God. But then when they reach a certain age, they become accountable for their beliefs, and if they die, they go to be with God only if they have said or done or believed the "right" things. Among those who believe this, this age of accountability is generally considered to be sometime around age twelve.

This belief raises a number of issues, one of them being the risk each new life faces. If every new baby being born could grow up to *not* believe the right things and go to hell forever, then prematurely terminating a child's life anytime from conception to twelve years of age would actually be the loving thing to do, guaranteeing that the child ends up in heaven, and not hell, forever. Why run the risk?

And that risk raises *another* question about this high-school student's death. What happens when a fifteen-year-old atheist dies? Was there a three-year window when he could have made a decision to change his eternal destiny? Did he miss his chance? What if he had lived to sixteen, and it was in that sixteenth year that

he came to believe what he was supposed to believe?
Was God limited to that three-year window, and if the
message didn't get to the young man in that time, well,
that's just unfortunate?

And what exactly would have had to happen in that
three-year window to change his future?

Would he have had to perform a specific rite or ritual?
Or take a class?
Or be baptized?
Or join a church?
Or have something happen somewhere in his heart?

Some believe he would have had to say a specific prayer.
Christians don't agree on exactly what this prayer is, but
for many the essential idea is that the only way to get
into heaven is to pray at some point in your life, asking
God to forgive you and telling God that you accept
Jesus, you believe Jesus died on the cross to pay the
price for your sins, and you want to go to heaven when
you die. Some call this "accepting Christ," others call
it the "sinner's prayer," and still others call it "getting
saved," being "born again," or being "converted."

That, of course, raises more questions. What about
people who have said some form of "the prayer" at some
point in their life, but it means nothing to them today?
What about those who said it in a highly emotionally
charged environment like a youth camp or church ser-

vice because it was the thing to do, but were unaware of the significance of what they were doing? What about people who have never said the prayer and don't claim to be Christians, but live a more Christlike life than some Christians?

This raises even more disconcerting questions about what the message even is. Some Christians believe and often repeat that all that matters is whether or not a person is going to heaven. Is that the message? Is that what life is about? Going somewhere else? If that's the gospel, the good news—if what Jesus does is get people *somewhere else*—then the central message of the Christian faith has very little to do with this life other than getting you what you need for the next one. Which of course raises the question: Is that the best God can do?

Which leads to a far more disturbing question. So is it true that the kind of person you are doesn't ultimately matter, as long as you've said or prayed or believed the right things? If you truly believed that, and you were surrounded by Christians who believed that, then you wouldn't have much motivation to do anything about the present suffering of the world, because you would believe you were going to leave someday and go *somewhere else* to be with Jesus. If this understanding of the good news of Jesus prevailed among Christians, the belief that Jesus's message is about how to get *somewhere else,* you could possibly end up with a world in which millions of people were starving, thirsty, and poor; the earth was being exploited and polluted; disease and despair were everywhere; and Christians weren't known for doing much about it. If it got bad enough, you might even have people rejecting Jesus because of how his followers lived.

That would be tragic.

One way to respond to these questions is with the clear, helpful answer: all that matters is how you respond to Jesus. And that answer totally resonates with me; it *is* about how you respond to Jesus. But it raises another important question: Which Jesus?

Renee Altson begins her book *Stumbling Toward Faith* with these words:

> I grew up in an abusive household. Much of my abuse was spiritual—and when I say spiritual, I don't mean new age, esoteric, random mumblings from half-Wiccan, hippie parents. . . . I mean that my father raped me while reciting the Lord's Prayer. I mean that my father molested me while singing Christian hymns.

That Jesus?

When one woman in our church invited her friend to come to one of our services, he asked her if it was a Christian church. She said yes, it was. He then told her about Christians in his village in eastern Europe who rounded up the Muslims in town and herded them into a building, where they opened fire on them with their machine guns and killed them all. He explained to her that he was a Muslim and had no interest in going to her Christian church.

That Jesus?

Or think about the many who know about Christians only from what they've seen on television and so assume that Jesus is antiscience, antigay, standing out on the sidewalk with his bullhorn, telling people that they're going to burn forever?

Those Jesuses?

Do you know any individuals who grew up in a Christian church and then walked away when they got older? Often pastors and parents and brothers and sisters are concerned about them and their spirituality—and often they should be. But sometimes those individuals' rejection of church and the Christian faith they were presented with as the only possible interpretation of what it means to follow Jesus may in fact be a sign of spiritual health. They may be resisting behaviors, interpretations, and attitudes that should be rejected. Perhaps they simply came to a point where they refused to accept the very sorts of things that Jesus would refuse to accept.

Some Jesuses should be rejected.

Often times when I meet atheists and we talk about the god they don't believe in, we quickly discover that I don't believe in that god either.

So when we hear that a certain person has "rejected Christ," we should first ask, "Which Christ?"

Many would respond to the question, "Which Jesus?" by saying that we have to trust that God will bring those who authentically represent the real Jesus into people's lives to show them the transforming truths of Jesus's life and message. A passage from Romans 10 is often quoted to explain this trust: "How can they hear without someone preaching to them?" And I wholeheartedly agree, but that raises another question. If our salvation, our future, our destiny is dependent on others bringing the message to us, teaching us, showing us—what happens if they don't do their part?

What if the missionary gets a flat tire?

This raises another, far more disturbing question:
Is your future in someone else's hands?

Which raises another question:
Is someone else's eternity resting in your hands?

So is it not only that a person has to respond, pray, accept, believe, trust, confess, and do—but also that someone else has to act, teach, travel, organize, fund-raise, and build so that the person can know what to respond, pray, accept, believe, trust, confess, and do?

At this point some would step in and remind us in the midst of all of these questions that it's not that complicated, and we have to remember that God has lots of ways of communicating apart from people speaking to each other face-to-face; the real issue, the one that can't be avoided, is whether a person has a "personal relationship" with God through Jesus. However that happens, whoever told whomever, however it was done, that's the bottom line: a personal relationship. If you don't have that, you will die apart from God and spend eternity in torment in hell.

The problem, however, is that the phrase "personal relationship" is found nowhere in the Bible.

Nowhere in the Hebrew scriptures, nowhere in the New Testament. Jesus never used the phrase. Paul didn't use it. Nor did John, Peter, James, or the woman who wrote the Letter to the Hebrews.

So if that's it,
if that's the point of it all,
if that's the ticket,

the center,
the one unavoidable reality,
the heart of the Christian faith,
why is it that no one used the phrase until the last
hundred years or so?

And that question raises another question. If the
message of Jesus is that God is offering the free gift of
eternal life through him—a gift we cannot earn by our
own efforts, works, or good deeds—and all we have to do
is accept and confess and believe, aren't those verbs?

And aren't verbs actions?

Accepting, confessing, believing—those are things we *do*.

Does that mean, then, that going to heaven is dependent
on something I do?

How is any of that grace?
How is that a gift?
How is that good news?

Isn't that what Christians have always claimed set their
religion apart—that it wasn't, in the end, a religion at
all—that you don't have to *do* anything, because God has
already done it through Jesus?

At this point another voice enters the discussion—the reasoned, wise voice of the one who reminds us that it is, after all, a story.

Just read the story, because a good story has a powerful way of rescuing us from abstract theological discussions that can tie us up in knots for years.

Excellent point.

In Luke 7 we read a story about a Roman centurion who sends a message to Jesus, telling him that all he has to do is say the word and the centurion's sick servant will be healed. Jesus is amazed at the man's confidence in him, and, turning to the crowd following him, he says, "I tell you, I have not found such great faith even in Israel."

Then in Luke 18, Jesus tells a story about two people who go to the temple to pray. The one prays about how glad he is to not be a sinner like other people, while the other stands at a distance and says, "God, have mercy on me, a sinner."

And then in Luke 23, the man hanging on the cross next to Jesus says to him, "Remember me when you come into your kingdom," and Jesus assures him that they'll be together in paradise.

So in the first story the centurion gives a speech about how authority works, in the second story the man praying asks for mercy, and in the third story the man asks to be remembered at a future date in time.

In the first case, Jesus isn't just accepting and approving; he's amazed.
And in the second case, he states that the man's words put him in better standing with God than God's own people.
And in the third case, the man is promised that later that very day he will be with Jesus in "paradise."

So is it what you say that saves you?

But then in John 3 Jesus tells a man named Nicodemus that if he wants to see the "kingdom of God" he must be "born again."

And in Luke 20, when Jesus is asked about the afterlife, he refers in his response to "those who are considered worthy of taking part in the age to come."

So is it about being born again
or being considered worthy?

Is it what you say
or what you are that saves you?

But then, in Matthew 6, Jesus is teaching his disciples how to pray, and he says that if they forgive others, then God will forgive them, and if they don't forgive others, then God won't forgive them.

Then in Matthew 7 Jesus explains, "Not everyone who says to me, 'Lord, Lord,' will enter the kingdom, but only those who do the will of my Father."

And then in Matthew 10 he teaches that "those who stand firm till the end will be saved."

So do we have to forgive others, do the will of the Father, or "stand firm" to be accepted by God?

Which is it?

Is it what we say,
or what we are,
or who we forgive,
or whether we do the will of God,
or if we "stand firm" or not?

But then in Luke 19, a man named Zacchaeus tells Jesus, "Here and now I give half of my possessions to the poor, and if I have cheated anybody out of anything, I will pay back four times the amount."

Jesus's response? "Today salvation has come to this house."

So is it what we say,
or is it who we are,
or is it what we do,
or is it what we say we're going to do?

And then in Mark 2, Jesus is teaching in a house and some men cut a hole in the roof and lower down their sick friend for Jesus to heal. When Jesus sees *their* faith, he says to the paralyzed man, "Son, your sins are forgiven."

His sins are forgiven because of *their* faith?

Is it what you say,
or who you are,
or what you do,
or what you say you're going to do,
or is it who your friends are or what your friends do?

But then in 1 Corinthians 7 it's written: "How do you know, wife, whether you will save your husband? Or, how do you know, husband, whether you will save your wife?" And then Paul writes in his first letter to Timothy that women "will be saved through childbearing" (chap. 2).

So is it what you say,
or who you are,
or what you do,
or what you say you're going to do,
or who your friends are,
or who you're married to,
or whether you give birth to children?

These questions bring us to one of the first "conversion" stories of the early church. We read in Acts 22 about a man named Saul (later, Paul) who is traveling to the city of Damascus to persecute Christians when he hears a voice ask him, "Why do you persecute me?"

He responds, "Who are you, Lord?"

The voice then replies: "I am Jesus of Nazareth, whom you are persecuting. . . . Get up and go into Damascus, and there you will be told all that you have been assigned to do."

That's his "conversion" experience?

Paul is asked a question.
Paul then asks a question in response to the question he's just been asked.
He's then told it's Jesus and he should go into the city and he'll know what to do.

Is it what you say,
or who you are,
or what you do,
or what you say you're going to do,
or who your friends are,
or who you're married to,
or whether you give birth to children?
Or is it what questions you're asked?
Or is it what questions you ask in return?

Or is it whether you do what you're told and go into the city?

And then in Romans 11, Paul writes, "And in this way all Israel will be saved."

All of Israel?
So is it the tribe, or family, or ethnic group you're born into?

But maybe all of these questions are missing the point. Let's set aside all of the saying and doing and being and cutting holes in roofs and assume it's more simple than that. As some would say, "Just believe."

In Luke 11, the Pharisees say that the only way that Jesus can drive out demons is that he's in league with the devil. Then in Mark 3, Jesus's family members come to get him because they think he's "out of his mind." And then in Matthew 16, when Jesus asks his disciples who people say he is, they tell him, "Some say John the Baptist; others say Elijah; and still others, Jeremiah or one of the prophets."

What we see in these passages and many others is that almost everybody, at least at first, has a difficult time grasping just who Jesus is.

Except for one particular group.

In Luke 4 a man possessed by an "evil spirit" yells at Jesus, "I know who you are—the Holy One of God!"

And in Matthew 8, when Jesus arrives on the shore in the region of the Gadarenes, the demon-possessed men shout at him, "What do you want with us, Son of God?"

And in Mark 1, Jesus wouldn't let demons speak, "because they knew who he was."

In the stories about Jesus a lot of people, including his own family, are uncertain about exactly who Jesus is and what he's up to—except demons, who know exactly who he is and what's he doing.

As James wrote: "You believe that there is one God. Good! Even the demons believe that—and shudder" (chap. 2).

And then in Luke 7, a woman who has lived a "sinful life" crashes a dinner Jesus is at and pours perfume on his feet after wetting his feet with her tears and drying them with her hair. Jesus then tells her that her "sins have been forgiven."

So demons believe,
and washing Jesus's feet with your tears gets your sins forgiven?

———————

We could go on,
verse after verse,
passage after passage,
question after question,
about heaven and hell and the afterlife
and salvation and believing and judgment
and who God is and what God is like
and how Jesus fits into any of it.

But this isn't just a book of questions.
It's a book of responses to these questions.

And so, away we go.
First, heaven.

CHAPTER 2

HERE IS THE NEW THERE

First,
heaven.

This is a photograph of a painting that hung on a wall in my grandmother's house from before I was born. As you can see, in the center of the picture is a massive cross, big enough for people to walk on. It hangs suspended in space, floating above an ominous red and black realm that threatens to swallow up whoever takes a wrong step. The people in the picture walking on the cross are clearly headed somewhere—and that somewhere is a city. A gleaming, bright city with a wall around it and lots of sunshine.

It's as if Thomas Kinkade and Dante were at a party, and one turned to the other sometime after midnight and uttered that classic line "You know, we really should work together sometime . . ."

When I asked my sister Ruth if she remembered this painting, she immediately replied, "Of course, it gave us all the creeps."

It's striking what we remember, isn't it? An image or idea can lodge itself in our consciousness to such a degree that, years later, it's still there. This is especially true when it comes to religion.

My wife, Kristen, and I often talk about raising our kids in such a way that they have as little as possible to *unlearn* later on in life.

One of the only violent images Jesus ever uses is when he speaks about those who cause children to stumble. With a shockingly hyperbolic flourish, he declares that the only fitting punishment is to tie a giant stone around their neck and throw them into the sea (Matt. 18).

Death by drowning—Jesus's idea of punishment for those who lead children astray. A haunting warning if there ever was one about the spongelike nature of a child's psyche.

I'm not saying that my grandma's painting did that, but it clearly unnerved at least two of us.

I show you this painting not because of its astounding ability to somehow fuse *Dungeons and Dragons,* Billy Graham, and that barbecue pit your uncle made out of half of a fifty-gallon barrel into one piece of art, but because this painting tells a story.

It's a story of movement,
from one place to the next,
from one realm to another,
from death to life,
with the cross as the bridge, the way, the hope.

From what we can see, the people in the painting are going somewhere, somewhere they've chosen to go, and they're leaving something behind so that they can go there.

But the story also tells us something else,
something really, really important,
something significant about location.
According to the painting,
all of this is happening *somewhere else.*

Giant crosses do not hang suspended in the air in the world that you and I call home. Cities do not float. And if you tripped and fell off the cross/sidewalk in this world, you would not free-fall indefinitely down into an abyss of giant red caves and hissing steam.

I show you this painting because, as surreal as it is, the fundamental story it tells about heaven—that it is *somewhere else*—is the story that many people know to be the Christian story.

Think of the cultural images that are associated with heaven: harps and clouds and streets of gold, everybody dressed in white robes.

(Does anybody look good in a white robe? Can you play sports in a white robe? How could it be heaven without sports? What about swimming? What if you spill food on the robe?)

Think of all of the jokes that begin with someone showing up at the gates of heaven, and St. Peter is there, like a bouncer at a club, deciding who does and doesn't get to enter.

For all of the questions and confusion about just what heaven is and who will be there, the one thing that appears to unite all of the speculation is the generally agreed-upon notion that heaven is, obviously, *somewhere else.*

And so the questions that are asked about heaven often have an otherworldly air to them:
What will we do all day?
Will we recognize people we used to know?

What will it be like?
Will there be dogs there?

I've heard pastors answer, "It will be unlike anything we can comprehend, like a church service that goes on forever," causing some to think, "That sounds more like hell."

And then there are those whose lessons about heaven consist primarily of who *will* be there and who *won't* be there. And so there's a woman sitting in a church service with tears streaming down her face, as she imagines being reunited with her sister who was killed in a car accident seventeen years ago. The woman sitting next to her, however, is realizing that if what the pastor is saying about heaven is true, she will be separated from her mother and father, brothers and sisters, cousins, aunts, uncles, and friends forever, with no chance of any reunion, ever. She in that very same moment has tears streaming down her face too, but they are tears of a different kind.

When she asks the pastor afterward if it's true that, because they aren't Christians none of her family will be there, she's told that she'll be having so much fun worshipping God that it won't matter to her. Which is quite troubling and confusing, because the people she loves the most in the world *do* matter to her.

Are there other ways to think about heaven, other than as that perfect floating shiny city hanging suspended there in the air above that ominous red and black realm with all that smoke and steam and hissing fire?

I say yes, there are.

In Matthew 19 a rich man asks Jesus: "Teacher, what good thing must I do to get eternal life?"

For some Christians, this is *the* question, the one that matters most. Compassion for the poor, racial justice, care for the environment, worship, teaching, and art are important, but in the end, for some followers of Jesus, they're not ultimately what it's all about.

It's "all about eternity," right?
Because that's what the bumper sticker says.

There are entire organizations with employees, websites, and newsletters devoted to training people to walk up to strangers in public places and ask them, "When you die and God asks you why you should be let into heaven, what will you say?" There are well-organized groups of Christians who go door-to-door asking people, "If you were to die tonight, where would you go?"

The rich man's question, then, is the perfect opportunity for Jesus to give a clear, straightforward answer to the only question that ultimately matters for many.

First, we can only assume, he'll correct the man's flawed understanding of how salvation works. He'll show the man how eternal life isn't something he has to earn or work for; it's a free gift of grace.

Then, he'll invite the man to confess, repent, trust, accept, and believe that Jesus has made a way for him to have a relationship with God.

Like any good Christian would.

Jesus, however, doesn't do any of that.

He asks the man: "Why do you ask me about what is good? There is only one who is good. If you want to enter life, keep the commandments."

"Enter life?"

Jesus refers to the man's intention as "entering life"? And then he tells him that you do *that* by keeping the commandments? This wasn't what Jesus was supposed to say.

The man, however, wants to know *which* of the commandments. There are 613 of them in the first five books of the Bible, so it's a fair question. In the culture Jesus lived in, an extraordinary amount of time was spent in serious discussion and debate about these 613 commandments, dissecting and debating just how to interpret and obey them.

Were some more important than others?
Could they be summarized?
What do you do when your donkey falls in a hole on the Sabbath?

Rescuing your donkey would be work, and that would be breaking the Sabbath commandment to rest, but there were also commands to protect and preserve life, including the life of donkeys, so what happens when obeying one commandment requires you to break another?

The Ten Commandments were central to this discussion because of the way in which they covered so many aspects of life in so few words. Jesus refers to them in answering the man's question about "which ones" by listing five of the Ten Commandments. But not just any five. The first four of the commandments were understood as dealing with our relationship with God— Jesus doesn't list any of those. The remaining six deal with our relationships with each other. Jesus mentions five of them, leaving one out.

The man hears Jesus's list of *five* and insists he's kept them all.

Jesus then tells him, "Go, sell your possessions, and give to the poor, and you will have treasure in heaven," which causes the man to walk away sad, "because he had great wealth."

Did we miss something?

The big words, the important words—"eternal life," "treasure," "heaven"—were all there in the conversation, but they weren't used in the ways that many Christians use them.

Shouldn't Jesus have given a clear answer to the man's obvious desire to know how to go to heaven when he dies? Is that why he walks away—because Jesus blew a perfectly good "evangelistic" opportunity? How does such a simple question—one Jesus could have answered so clearly from a Christian perspective—turn into such a convoluted dialogue involving commandments and treasures and wealth and ending with the man walking away?

The answer,
it turns out,
is in the question.

When the man asks about getting "eternal life," he isn't asking about how to go to heaven when he dies. This wasn't a concern for the man or Jesus. This is why Jesus doesn't tell people how to "go to heaven." It wasn't what Jesus came to do.

Heaven, for Jesus, was deeply connected with what he called "this age" and "the age to come."

In Matthew 13 Jesus speaks of a harvest at the "end of the age," and in Luke 20 he teaches about "the people of this age" and some who are "considered worthy of taking part in the age to come." Sometimes he describes the age to come simply as "entering life," as in Mark 9—"it's better for you to enter life maimed"—and other times he teaches that by standing firm "you will win life [in the age to come]," as in Luke 21. And then, just before he leaves his disciples in Matthew 28, Jesus reassures them that he is with them "always, to the very end of the age."

Jesus's disciples ask him in Matthew 24, "What will be the sign of your coming and of the end of the age?" because this is how they had been taught to think about things—
this age,
and then the age to come.

We might call them "eras" or "periods of time":
this age—the one we're living in—and the age to come.

Another way of saying "life in the age to come" in Jesus's day was to say "eternal life." In Hebrew the phrase is *olam habah.*

What must I do to inherit *olam habah*?

This age,
and the one to come,
the one *after* this one.

When the wealthy man walks away from Jesus, Jesus turns to his disciples and says to them, "No one who has left home or wife or brothers or sisters or parents or children, for the sake of the kingdom of God will fail to receive many times as much in this age, and in the age to come eternal life" (Luke 18).

Now, the English word "age" here is the word *aion* in New Testament Greek. *Aion* has multiple meanings—one we'll look at here, and another we'll explore later. One meaning of *aion* refers to a period of time, as in "The spirit of the age" or "They were gone for ages." When we use the word "age" like this, we are referring less to a precise measurement of time, like an hour or a day or a year, and more to a period or era of time. This is crucial to our understanding of the word *aion,* because it doesn't mean "forever" as we think of forever. When we say "forever," what we are generally referring to is something that will go on, year after 365-day year, never ceasing in

the endless unfolding of segmented, measurable units
of time, like a clock that never stops ticking. That's not
this word. The first meaning of this word *aion* refers to a
period of time with a beginning and an end.

So according to Jesus there is this age, this *aion*—
the one they, and we, are living in—
and then a coming age,
also called "the world to come"
or simply "eternal life."

Seeing the present and future in terms of two ages was
not a concept or teaching that originated with Jesus.
He came from a long line of prophets who had been
talking about life in the age to come for hundreds of
years before him. They believed that history was headed
somewhere—not just their history as a tribe and nation,
but the history of the entire universe—because they
believed that God had not abandoned the world and that
a new day, a new age, a new era was coming.

The prophet Isaiah said that in that new day
"the nations will stream to" Jerusalem,
and God will
"settle disputes for many peoples";
people will "beat their swords into plowshares
and their spears into pruning hooks" (chap. 2).

As we would say,
peace on earth.

Isaiah said that everybody will walk
"in the light of the LORD"
and
"they will neither harm nor destroy"
in that day.

The earth, Isaiah said, will be
"filled with the knowledge of the LORD
as the waters cover the sea" (chap. 11).
He described
"a feast of rich food for all peoples"
because God will
"destroy the shroud that enfolds all peoples,
the sheet that covers all nations,
he will swallow up death forever."
God "will wipe away the tears from all faces";
and "remove his people's disgrace from all the earth"
(chap. 25).

The prophet Ezekiel said that people will be given
grain and fruit and crops and new hearts and new spirits
(chap. 36).

The prophet Amos promised that everything will be
repaired and restored and rebuilt and
"new wine will drip from the mountains" (chap. 9).

Life in the age to come.
If this sounds like heaven on earth,
that's because it is.
Literally.

A couple of observations about the prophets' promises regarding life in the age to come.

First, they spoke about "all the nations." That's *everybody.* That's all those different skin colors, languages, dialects, and accents; all those kinds of food and music; all those customs, habits, patterns, clothing, traditions, and ways of celebrating—
multiethnic,
multisensory,
multieverything.

That's an extraordinarily complex, interconnected, and diverse reality, a reality in which individual identities aren't lost or repressed, but embraced and celebrated. An expansive unity that goes beyond and yet fully embraces staggering levels of diversity.

A racist would be miserable in the world to come.

Second, one of the most striking aspects of the pictures the prophets used to describe this reality is how earthy it is. Wine and crops and grain and people and feasts and buildings and homes. It's *here* they were talking about, this world, the one we know—but rescued, transformed, and renewed.

When Isaiah predicted that spears would become pruning hooks, that's a reference to cultivating. Pruning and trimming and growing and paying close attention to the plants and whether they're getting enough water and if their roots are deep enough. Soil under the fingernails, grapes being trampled under bare feet, fingers sticky from handling fresh fruit.

It's that green stripe you get around the sole of your shoes when you mow the lawn.

Life in the age to come.
Earthy.

Third, much of their vision of life in the age to come was not new. Deep in their bones was the Genesis story of Adam and Eve, who were turned loose in a garden to name the animals and care for the earth and enjoy it.

To name is to order, to participate, to partner with God in taking the world somewhere.

"Here it is,
a big, beautiful, fascinating world,"
God says.
"Do something with it!"

For there to be new wine, someone has to crush the grapes.
For the city to be rebuilt, someone has to chop down the trees to make the beams to construct the houses.

For there to be no more war, someone has to take the sword and get it hot enough in the fire to hammer into the shape of a plow.

This participation is important, because Jesus and the prophets lived with an awareness that God has been looking for partners since the beginning, people who will take seriously their divine responsibility to care for the earth and each other in loving, sustainable ways. They centered their hopes in the God who simply does not give up on creation and the people who inhabit it. The God who is the source of all life, who works from within creation to make something new. The God who can do what humans cannot. The God who gives new spirits and new hearts and new futures.

Central to their vision of human flourishing in God's renewed world, then, was the prophets' announcement that a number of things that can survive in this world will not be able to survive in the world to come.
Like war.
Rape.
Greed.
Injustice.
Violence.
Pride.
Division.
Exploitation.
Disgrace.

Their description of life in the age to come is both thrilling and unnerving at the same time. For the earth to be free of anything destructive or damaging, certain things have to be banished. Decisions have to be made. Judgments have to be rendered. And so they spoke of a cleansing, purging, decisive day when God would make those judgments. They called this day the "day of the LORD."

The day when God says "ENOUGH!" to anything that threatens the peace (*shalom* is the Hebrew word), harmony, and health that God intends for the world.

God says no to injustice.
God says, "Never again" to the oppressors who prey on the weak and vulnerable.
God declares a ban on weapons.

It's important to remember this the next time we hear people say they can't believe in a "God of judgment."

Yes, they can.
Often, we can think of little else.
Every oil spill,
every report of another woman sexually assaulted,
every news report that another political leader has silenced the opposition through torture, imprisonment, and execution,

every time we see someone stepped on by an institution
or corporation more interested in profit than people,
every time we stumble upon one more instance of the
human heart gone wrong,
we shake our fist and cry out,
"Will somebody please do something about this?"

We crave judgment,
we long for it,
we thirst for it.
Bring it,
unleash it,
as the prophet Amos says,
"Let justice roll on like a river" (chap. 5).

Same with the word "anger." When we hear people
saying they can't believe in a God who gets angry—yes,
they can. How should God react to a child being forced
into prostitution? How should God feel about a country
starving while warlords hoard the food supply? What
kind of God wouldn't get angry at a financial scheme that
robs thousands of people of their life savings?

And that is the promise of the prophets in the age to
come:
God acts.
Decisively.
On behalf of everybody
who's ever been stepped on by the machine,
exploited,

abused,
forgotten,
or mistreated.
God puts an end to it.
God says, "Enough."

Of course, to celebrate this, anticipate this, and find
ourselves thrilled by this promise of the world made right
brings with it the haunting thought that we each know
what lurks in our own heart—
our role in corrupting this world,
the litany of ways in which our own sins have contributed
to the heartbreak we're surrounded by,
all those times we hardened our heart and kept right on
walking,
ignoring the cry of someone in need.

And so in the midst of prophets' announcements about
God's judgment we also find promises about mercy and
grace.
Isaiah quotes God, saying, "Come, . . . though your sins
are like scarlet, they shall be as white as snow" (chap. 1).

Justice and mercy hold hands,
they kiss,
they belong together in the age to come,
an age that is complex, earthy, participatory, and free
from all death, destruction, and despair.

When we talk about heaven, then, or eternal life, or the afterlife—any of that—it's important that we begin with the categories and claims that people were familiar with in Jesus's first-century Jewish world. They did not talk about a future life *somewhere else,* because they anticipated a coming day when the world would be restored, renewed, and redeemed and there would be peace on earth.

So when the man asks Jesus how he can get eternal life, Jesus is not surprised or caught off guard by the man's question, because this was one of the most important things people were talking about in Jesus's day.

How do you make sure you'll be a part of the new thing God is going to do? How do you best become the kind of person whom God could entrust with significant responsibility in the age to come?

The standard answer was: live the commandments. God has shown you how to live. Live that way. The more you become a person of peace and justice and worship and generosity, the more actively you participate now in ordering and working to bring about God's kind of world, the more ready you will be to assume an even greater role in the age to come.

But Jesus is aware that something is wrong with the man. Rich people were rare at that time, so there is good reason to believe that Jesus knew something about him and his reputation. Jesus mentions five, not six, of the commandments about relationship with others. He leaves out the last command, which prohibited coveting. To covet is to crave what someone else has. Coveting is the disease of always wanting more, and it's rooted in a profound dissatisfaction with the life God has given you. Coveting is what happens when you aren't at peace.

The man says he's kept all of the commandments that Jesus mentions, but Jesus hasn't mentioned the one about coveting. Jesus then tells him to sell his possessions and give the money to the poor, which Jesus doesn't tell other people, because it's not an issue for them. It is, for this man. The man is greedy—and greed has no place in the world to come. He hasn't learned yet that he has a sacred calling to use his wealth to move creation forward. How can God give him more responsibility and resources in the age to come, when he hasn't handled well what he's been given in this age?

Jesus promises him that if he can do it, if he can trust God to liberate him from his greed, he'll have "treasure in heaven."

The man can't do it, and so he walks away.

Jesus takes the man's question about his life *then* and makes it about the kind of life he's living *now.* Jesus drags the future into the present, promising the man that there will be treasure in heaven for him if he can do it.

All of which raises the question: What does Jesus mean when he uses that word "heaven"?

———

First, there was tremendous respect in the culture that Jesus lived in for the name of God—so much so that many wouldn't even say it. That is true to this day. I occasionally receive e-mails and letters from people who spell the name "G-d." In Jesus's day, one of the ways that people got around actually saying the name of God was to substitute the word "heaven" for the word "God." Jesus often referred to the "kingdom of heaven," and he tells stories about people "sinning against heaven." "Heaven" in these cases is simply another way of saying "God."

Second, Jesus consistently affirmed heaven as a real place, space, and dimension of God's creation, where God's will and only God's will is done. Heaven is that realm where things are as God intends them to be.

On earth, lots of wills are done.
Yours, mine, and many others.
And so, at present, heaven and earth are not one.

What Jesus taught,
what the prophets taught,
what all of Jewish tradition pointed to
and what Jesus lived in anticipation of,
was the day when earth and heaven would be one.

The day when God's will would be done on earth
as it is now done in heaven.
The day when earth and heaven *will be the same place.*

This is the story of the Bible.
This is the story Jesus lived and told.
As it's written at the end of the Bible in Revelation 21:
"God's dwelling place is now among the people."

Life in the age to come.

This is why Jesus tells the man that if he sells his
possessions, he'll have rewards in heaven. Rewards are a
dynamic rather than a static reality. Many people think of
heaven, and they picture mansions (a word nowhere in
the Bible's descriptions of heaven) and Ferraris and literal
streets of gold, as if the best God can come up with is
Beverly Hills in the sky. Tax-free, of course, and without
the smog.

But those are static images—fixed, flat, unchanging. A car
is a car is a car; same with a mansion. They are the same,
day after day after day, give or take a bit of wear and
tear.

There's even a phrase about doing a good deed. People
will say that it earns you "another star in your crown."

(By the way, when the writer John in the book of
Revelation gets a current glimpse of the heavens, one

detail he mentions about crowns is that people are
taking them off [chap. 4]. Apparently, in the unvarnished
presence of the divine a lot of things that we consider
significant turn out to be, much like wearing a crown,
quite absurd.)

But a crown, much like a mansion or a car, is a
possession. There's nothing wrong with possessions; it's
just that they have value to us only when we use them,
engage them, and enjoy them. They're nouns that mean
something only in conjunction with verbs.

That's why wealth is so dangerous: if you're not careful
you can easily end up with a garage full of nouns.

In the Genesis poem that begins the Bible, life is a
pulsing, progressing, evolving, dynamic reality in which
tomorrow will not be a repeat of today, because things
are, at the most fundamental level of existence, going
somewhere.

When Jesus tells the man that there are rewards for him,
he's promising the man that receiving the peace of God
now, finding gratitude for what he does have, and sharing
it with those who need it will create in him all the more
capacity for joy in the world to come.

How we think about heaven, then, directly affects how
we understand what we do with our days and energies
now, in this age. Jesus teaches us how to live now in such

a way that what we create, who we give our efforts to, and how we spend our time will all endure in the new world.

Taking heaven seriously, then, means taking suffering seriously, now. Not because we've bought into the myth that we can create a utopia given enough time, technology, and good voting choices, but because we have great confidence that God has not abandoned human history and is actively at work within it, taking it somewhere.

Around a billion people in the world today do not have access to clean water. People will have access to clean water in the age to come, and so working for clean-water access for all is participating now in the life of the age to come.

That's what happens when the future is dragged into the present.

It often appears that those who talk the most about going to heaven when you die talk the least about bringing heaven to earth right now, as Jesus taught us to pray: "Your will be done on earth as it is in heaven." At the same time, it often appears that those who talk the most about relieving suffering now talk the least about heaven when we die.

Jesus teaches us to pursue the life of heaven now and also then, anticipating the day when earth and heaven are one.

Honest business,
redemptive art,
honorable law,
sustainable living,
medicine,
education,
making a home,
tending a garden—
they're all sacred tasks to be done in partnership with God now, because they will all go on in the age to come.

In heaven,
on earth.

Our eschatology shapes our ethics.
Eschatology is about last things.
Ethics are about how you live.

What you believe about the future shapes, informs, and determines how you live now.

If you believe that you're going to leave and evacuate to *somewhere else,* then why do anything about this world? A proper view of heaven leads not to escape from the world, but to full engagement with it, all with the anticipation of a coming day when things are on earth as they currently are in heaven.

When Jesus tells the man he will have treasure in heaven, he's promising the man that taking steps to be free of his greed—in this case, selling his possessions—will open him up to more and more participation in God's new world, the one that was breaking into human history with Jesus himself.

In Matthew 20 the mother of two of Jesus's disciples says to Jesus, "Grant that one of these two sons of mine may sit at your right and other at your left in your kingdom." She doesn't want bigger mansions or larger piles of gold for them, because static images of wealth and prosperity were not what filled people's heads when they thought of heaven in her day. She understood heaven to be about partnering with God to make a new and better world, one with increasingly complex and expansive expressions and dimensions of *shalom,* creativity, beauty, and design.

So when people ask, "What will we do in heaven?" one possible answer is to simply ask: "What do you love to do now that will go on in the world to come?"

What is it that when you do it, you lose track of time because you get lost in it? What do you do that makes you think, "I could do this forever"? What is it that makes you think, "I was made for this"?

If you ask these kinds of questions long enough you will find some impulse related to creation. Some way to be, something to do. Heaven is both the peace, stillness, serenity, and calm that come from having everything in its right place—that state in which nothing is required, needed, or missing—and the endless joy that comes from participating in the ongoing creation of the world.

The pastor John writes in Revelation 20 that people will reign with God. The word "reign" means "to actively participate in the ordering of creation." We were made to explore and discover and learn and create and shape and form and engage this world.

This helps us understand the exchange between the rich man and Jesus. Jesus wants to free him to more actively participate in God's good world, but the man isn't up for it.

And his unwillingness, we learn, leads us to another insight about heaven.

Heaven comforts, but it also confronts.
The prophets promised a new world free from tears and pain and harm and disgrace and disease. That's comforting. And people have clung to those promises for years, because they're inspiring and can help sustain us through all kinds of difficulties.

But heaven also confronts. Heaven, we learn, has teeth, flames, edges, and sharp points. What Jesus is insisting with the rich man is that certain things simply will not survive in the age to come. Like coveting. And greed. The one thing people won't be wanting in the perfect peace and presence of God is someone else's life. The man is clearly attached to his wealth and possessions, so much so that when Jesus invites him to leave them behind, he can't do it.

Jesus brings the man hope, but that hope bears within it judgment.

The man's heart is revealed through his response to Jesus's invitation to sell his things, and his heart is hard. His attachment to his possessions is revealed, and he clings all the more tightly.

The apostle Paul writes in 1 Corinthians 3 that "the Day" the prophets spoke of, the one that inaugurates life in the age to come, will "bring everything to light" and "reveal it with fire," the kind of fire that will "test the quality of each person's work." Some in this process will find that they spent their energies and efforts on things that won't be in heaven-on-earth. "If it is burned up," Paul writes, "the builder will suffer loss but yet will be saved, even though only as one escaping through the flames."

Flames in heaven.

Imagine being a racist in heaven-on-earth, sitting down at the great feast and realizing that you're sitting next to *them*. *Those* people. The ones you've despised for years. Your racist attitude would simply not survive. Those flames in heaven would be hot.

Jesus makes no promise that in the blink of an eye we will suddenly become totally different people who have vastly different tastes, attitudes, and perspectives. Paul makes it very clear that we will have our true selves revealed and that once the sins and habits and bigotry and pride and petty jealousies are prohibited and removed, for some there simply won't be much left. "As one escaping through the flames" is how he put it.

It's very common to hear talk about heaven framed in terms of who "gets in" or how to "get in." What we find Jesus teaching, over and over and over again, is that he's interested in our hearts being transformed, so that we can actually handle heaven. To portray heaven as bliss, peace, and endless joy is a beautiful picture, but it raises the question: How many of us could handle it, as we are today? How would we each do in a reality that had no capacity for cynicism or slander or worry or pride?

It's important, then, to keep in mind that heaven has the potential to be a kind of starting over. Learning how to be human all over again. Imagine living with no fear.

Ever. That would take some getting used to. So would a world where loving your neighbor was the only option. So would a world where every choice was good for the earth. That would be a strange world at first. That could take some getting used to.

Jesus called disciples—students of life—to learn from him how to live in God's world God's way. Constantly learning and growing and evolving and absorbing. Tomorrow is never simply a repeat of today.

Much of the speculation about heaven—and, more important, the confusion—comes from the idea that in the blink of an eye we will automatically become totally different people who "know" everything. But our heart, our character, our desires, our longings—those things take time.

Jesus calls disciples in order to teach us how to be and what to be; his intention is for us to be growing progressively in generosity, forgiveness, honesty, courage, truth telling, and responsibility, so that as these take over our lives we are taking part more and more and more in life in the age to come, now.

The flames of heaven, it turns out, lead us to the surprise of heaven. Jesus tells a story in Matthew 25 about people invited into "the kingdom prepared for [them] since the creation of the world," and their first reaction is . . . surprise.

They start asking questions, trying to figure it out. Interesting, that. It's not a story of people boldly walking in through the pearly gates, confident that, because of their faith, beliefs, or even actions, they'll be welcomed in. It's a story about people saying,

"What?"

"Us?"

"When did we ever see you?"

"What did we ever do to deserve it?"

In other stories he tells, very religious people who presume that they're "in" hear from him: "I never knew you. Away from me, you evildoers!" (Matt. 7).

Heaven, it turns out, is full of the unexpected.

In a story Jesus tells in Luke 18 about two men going up to the temple to pray, it's the "sinner," the "unrighteous man," who goes home justified, while the faithful, observant religious man is harshly judged.

Again, surprise.

Jesus tells another story about a great banquet a man gave (Luke 14). The people who were invited, those who would normally attend such a feast, had better things to do. So, in their absence, the host invites all of the people from the streets and alleyways who would never attend a party like this.

Unexpected, surprising—not what you'd think. These aren't isolated impulses in Jesus's outlook; they're the themes he comes back to again and again. He tells entire villages full of extremely devoted religious people that they're in danger, while seriously questionable "sinners" will be better off than them "in that day."

Think about the single mom, trying to raise kids, work multiple jobs, and wrangle child support out of the kids' father, who used to beat her. She's faithful, true, and utterly devoted to her children. In spite of the circumstances, she never loses hope that they can be raised in love and go on to break the cycle of dysfunction and abuse. She never goes out, never takes a vacation, never has enough money to buy anything for herself. She gets a few hours of sleep and then repeats the cycle of cooking, work, laundry, bills, more work, until she falls into bed late at night, exhausted.

With what she has been given she has been faithful. She is a woman of character and substance. She never gives up. She is kind and loving even when she's exhausted.

She can be trusted.
Is she the last who Jesus says will be first?

Does God say to her, "You're the kind of person I can run the world with"?

Think about her, and then think about the magazines that line the checkout aisles at most grocery stores. The faces on the covers are often of beautiful, rich, famous, talented people embroiled in endless variations of scandal and controversy.

Where did they spend those millions of dollars?
What did they do with those talents?
How did they use their influence?

Did they use any of it to help create the new world God is making?
Or are we seeing the first who will be last that Jesus spoke of?

When it comes to people, then—the *who* of heaven—what Jesus does again and again is warn us against rash judgments about who's in and who's out.

But the surprise isn't just regarding the *who;*
it's also about the *when* of heaven.

Jesus is hanging on the cross between two insurgents when one of them says to him, "Remember me when you come into your kingdom."

Notice that the man doesn't ask to go to heaven. He doesn't ask for his sins to be forgiven. He doesn't invite

Jesus into his heart. He doesn't announce that he now believes.

He simply asks to be remembered by Jesus in the age to come.

He wants to be a part of it. Of course.
Jesus assures him that he'll be with him in paradise . . .
that day. The man hadn't asked about *today;* he had
asked about *that day.* He believes that God is doing
something new through Jesus and he wants to be a part
of it, whenever it is.

And that's all Jesus needs to hear to promise him
"paradise" later that day. Just around the corner. In a few
hours.

According to Jesus, then, heaven is as far away as that
day when heaven and earth become one again and as
close as a few hours.

The apostle Paul writes to the Philippians that either he
would go on living, or he would be killed and immediately
be with Christ (chap. 1).

Paul believed that there is a dimension of creation,
a place, a space, a realm beyond the one we currently
inhabit

and yet near and connected with it.
He writes of getting glimpses of it,
being a citizen of it,
and being there the moment he dies.

Paul writes to the Corinthians about two kinds of bodies.
The first is the kind we each inhabit now, the kind that
gets old and weary and eventually gives out on us. The
second kind is one he calls "imperishable" (1 Cor. 15),
one immune to the ravages of time, one we'll receive
when heaven and earth are one. Prior to that, then, after
death we are without a body. In heaven, but without a
body. A body is of the earth. Made of dust. Part of this
creation, not that one. Those currently "in heaven" are
not, obviously, here. And so they're with God, but without
a body.

These truths, about the present incompleteness of both
earth and heaven, lead us to another truth about heaven:

Heaven, for Jesus, wasn't *less* real, but *more* real.

The dominant cultural assumptions and
misunderstandings about heaven have been at work for
so long, it's almost automatic for many to think of heaven
as ethereal, intangible, esoteric, and immaterial.

Floaty, dreamy, hazy.
Somewhere else.

People in white robes with perfect hair floating by on clouds, singing in perfect pitch.

But for Jesus, heaven is more real than what we experience now. This is true for the future, when earth and heaven become one, but also for today.

To understand this, let's return to that Greek word *aion,* the one that we translate as "age" in English. We saw earlier how *aion* refers to a period of time with a beginning and an end. Another meaning of *aion* is a bit more complex and nuanced, because it refers to a particular *intensity of experience that transcends time.*

Remember sitting in class, and it was so excruciatingly boring that you found yourself staring at the clock? Tick. Tick. Tick. What happened to time in those moments? It slowed down. We even say, "It felt like it was taking *forever.*" Now when we use the word "forever" in this way, we are not talking about a 365-day year followed by a 365-day year followed by another 365-day year, and so on. What we are referring to is the intensity of feeling in that moment. That agonized boredom caused time to appear to bend and twist and warp.

Another example, this one less about agony and more about ecstasy. When you fall in love, those first conversations can take hours and yet they feel like minutes. You're so caught up in being with that person that you lose track of time. In that case, the clock doesn't slow down; instead, time "flies."

Whether an experience is pleasurable or painful, in the extreme moments of life what we encounter is time dragging and flying, slowing down and speeding up. That's what *aion* refers to—a particularly intense experience. *Aion* is often translated as "eternal" in English, which is an altogether different word from "forever."

Let me be clear: heaven is not forever in the way that we think of forever, as a uniform measurement of time, like days and years, marching endlessly into the future. That's not a category or concept we find in the Bible. This is why a lot of translators choose to translate *aion* as "eternal." By this they don't mean the literal passing of time; they mean transcending time, belonging to another realm altogether.

To summarize, then, sometimes when Jesus used the word "heaven," he was simply referring to God, using the word as a substitute for the name of God.
Second, sometimes when Jesus spoke of heaven, he was referring to the future coming together of heaven and earth in what he and his contemporaries called life in the age to come.
And then third—and this is where things get really, really interesting—when Jesus talked about heaven, he was talking about our present *eternal, intense, real*

experiences of joy, peace, and love in this life, this side of death *and* the age to come. Heaven for Jesus wasn't just "someday"; it was a present reality. Jesus blurs the lines, inviting the rich man, and us, into the merging of heaven and earth, the future and present, *here* and *now.*

To say it again, eternal life is less about a kind of time that starts when we die, and more about a quality and vitality of life lived now in connection to God.

Eternal life doesn't start when we die;
It starts now.
It's not about a life that begins at death;
it's about experiencing the kind of life now that can endure and survive even death.

We live in several dimensions.
Up and down.
Left and right.
Forward and backward.
Three to be exact.

And yet we've all had experiences when those three dimensions weren't adequate. Moments when we were acutely, overwhelmingly aware of other realities just beyond this one.

At the front edge of science string theorists are now telling us that they can show the existence of at least eleven dimensions. If we count time as the fourth dimension, that's seven dimensions beyond what we now know.

So there's left and right, and up and down, and front and back.
Got that.
But is there also
in . . . ?
and out . . . ?
or around . . . ?
and through . . . ?
or between . . . ?
or beside . . . ?
or beyond . . . ?

Jesus talked about a reality he called the kingdom of God. He described an all-pervasive dimension of being, a bit like oxygen for us or water for a fish, that he insisted was here, at hand, now, among us, and upon us. He spoke with God as if God was right here, he healed with power that he claimed was readily accessible all the time, and he taught his disciples that they would do even greater things than what they saw him doing. He spoke of oneness with God, the God who is so intimately connected with life in this world that every hair on your head is known. Jesus lived and spoke as if the whole world was a thin place for him, with endless dimensions of the divine infinitesimally close, with every moment and every location simply another experience of the divine reality that is all around us, through us, under and above us all the time.

It's as if we're currently trying to play the piano while wearing oven mitts.

We can make a noise, sometimes even hit the notes well enough to bang out a melody, but it doesn't sound like it could, or should.

The elements are all there—fingers, keys, strings, ears—but there's something in the way, something inhibiting our ability to fully experience all the possibilities. The apostle Paul writes that now we see "as in a mirror; then we shall see face to face" (1 Cor. 13).

Right now, we're trying to embrace our lover, but we're wearing a hazmat suit.
We're trying to have a detailed conversation about complex emotions, but we're underwater.
We're trying to taste the thirty-two different spices in the curry, but our mouth is filled with gravel.

Yes, there is plenty in the scriptures about life in the age to come, about our resurrected, heaven-and-earth-finally-come-together-as-one body, a body that's been "clothed in the immortal" that will make this body, the one we inhabit at this moment, seem like a temporary tent.

And yes, there were plenty of beliefs then about what the future would hold, just as there are now.

But when Jesus talks with the rich man, he has one thing in mind: he wants the man to experience the life of heaven, eternal life, "*aion*ian" life, now. For that man, his wealth was in the way; for others it's worry or stress or pride or envy—the list goes on. We know that list.

Jesus invites us,
in this life,
in this broken, beautiful world,
to experience the life of heaven now.
He insisted over and over that God's peace, joy, and love are currently available to us, exactly as we are.

So how do I answer questions about heaven?
How would I summarize all that Jesus teaches?

There's heaven now, somewhere else.
There's heaven here, sometime else.
And then there's Jesus's invitation to heaven
here
and
now,
in this moment,
in this place.

Try and paint *that*.

not bad!

CHAPTER 3

HELL

First, heaven.
Now, hell.

Several years ago I was getting ready to speak in San Francisco when I was told that there were protestors on the sidewalk in front of the theater. They were telling the people standing in line waiting to get in that they were in serious trouble with God because they had come to hear me talk. A friend of mine thought it would be fun to get pictures of the protesters. When he showed them to me later, I noticed that one of the protestors had a jacket on with these words stitched on the back:

"Turn or Burn."

That about sums it up, doesn't it?

Fury, wrath, fire, torment, judgment, eternal agony, endless anguish.

Hell.

That's all part of the story, right?
Trust God, accept Jesus, confess, repent, and everything will go well for you. But if you don't, well, the Bible is quite clear . . .

Sin, refuse to repent, harden your heart, reject Jesus, and when you die, it's over. Or actually, the torture and anguish and eternal torment will have just begun.

That's how it is—because that's what God is like, correct? God is loving and kind and full of grace and mercy— unless there isn't confession and repentance and salvation in this lifetime, at which point God punishes forever. That's the Christian story, right?

Is that what Jesus taught?

To answer that question, I want to show you every single verse in the Bible in which we find the actual word "hell."

First, the Hebrew scriptures. There isn't an exact word or concept in the Hebrew scriptures for hell other than a few words that refer to death and the grave.

One of them is the Hebrew word "Sheol," a dark, mysterious, murky place people go when they die, as in Psalm 18: "The cords of Sheol entangled me" (NRSV). There's also mention of "the depths," as in Psalm 30: "I will exalt you, LORD, for you lifted me out of the depths"; the "pit," as in Psalm 103: "The LORD . . . who redeems your life from the pit"; and the grave, as in Psalm 6: "Who praises you from the grave?"

There are a few references to the realm of the dead, as in Psalm 16: "My body also will rest secure, because you will not abandon me to the realm of the dead," but as far as meanings go, that's the extent of what we find in the Hebrew scriptures.

So what do we learn?

First, we consistently find affirmations of the power of God over all of life and death, as in 1 Samuel 2: "The Lord brings death and makes alive; he brings down to the grave and raises up"; and Deuteronomy 32: "There is no god besides me. I put to death and I bring to life."

We do find several affirmations of God's presence and involvement in whatever it is that happens after a person dies, although it's fairly ambiguous at best as to just what exactly that looks like.

In one of the stories about Moses, God is identified as the God of "Abraham, Isaac, and Jacob." Those three—

Abraham, Isaac, and Jacob—were dead by the time this story about Moses takes place. *Where* exactly Abraham, Isaac, and Jacob were at that time isn't mentioned, but Moses is told that God is still their God (Exod. 3).

Once again, it's an affirmation of God's enduring and sustaining power over life and death, and yet very little is given in the way of actual details regarding individual destinies.

Second, the Hebrews often used the words "life" and "death" in a different sense than we do. We're used to people speaking of life and death as fixed states or destinations, as in you're either alive or you're dead. What we find in the scriptures is a more nuanced understanding that sees life and death as two ways of being alive. When Moses in Deuteronomy 30 calls the Hebrews to choose life over death, he's not forcing them to decide whether they will be killed on the spot; he's confronting them with their choice of the kind of life they're going to keep on living. The one kind of life is in vital connection with the living God, in which they experience more and more peace and wholeness. The other kind of life is less and less connected with God and contains more and more despair and destruction.

Third, it's important here to remember that the Israelites, who wrote the Hebrew scriptures, had been oppressed and enslaved by their neighbors the Egyptians, who built pyramids and ornate coffins and buried themselves in rooms filled with gold, because of their beliefs about life after death. Those beliefs appear to have been a turnoff for the Jews, who were far more interested in the ethics of and ways of living *this* life.

There is a story about the death of King David's child, in which David says that if he can't bring the child back, he would go to where the child is (2 Sam. 12). There are several mentions in the book of Job about lying down, descending, and being buried in the dust—all references to death.

But, simply put, the Hebrew commentary on what happens after a person dies isn't very articulated or defined. Sheol, death, and the grave in the consciousness of the Hebrew writers are all a bit vague and "underworldly." For whatever reasons, the precise details of who goes where, when, how, with what, and for how long simply aren't things the Hebrew writers were terribly concerned with.

Next, then, the New Testament. The actual word "hell" is used roughly twelve times in the New Testament, almost exclusively by Jesus himself. The Greek word that gets translated as "hell" in English is the word "Gehenna." *Ge* means "valley," and *henna* means "Hinnom." Gehenna, the Valley of Hinnom, was an actual valley on the south and west side of the city of Jerusalem.

Gehenna, in Jesus's day, was the city dump.

People tossed their garbage and waste into this valley.
There was a fire there, burning constantly to consume
the trash. Wild animals fought over scraps of food along
the edges of the heap. When they fought, their teeth
would make a gnashing sound. Gehenna was the place
with the gnashing of teeth, where the fire never went out.

Gehenna was an actual place that Jesus's listeners would
have been familiar with. So the next time someone asks
you if you believe in an actual hell, you can always say,
"Yes, I do believe that my garbage goes somewhere . . ."

James uses the word "Gehenna" once in his letter to refer
to the power of the tongue (chap. 3), but otherwise all of
the mentions are from Jesus.

Jesus says in Matthew 5, "Anyone who says, 'You fool!'
will be in danger of the fire of hell," and "It is better for
you to lose one part of your body than for your whole
body to be thrown into hell." In Matthew 10 and Luke 12
he says, "Be afraid of the One who can destroy both soul
and body in hell," and in Matthew 18 and Mark 9 he says,
"It is better for you to enter life with one eye than to have
two eyes and be thrown into the fire of hell." In Matthew
23 he tells very committed religious leaders that they win
converts and make them "twice as much a child of hell"
as they are, and then he asks them, "How will you escape
being condemned to hell?"

Gehenna,
the town garbage pile.

And that's it.
Those are all of the mentions of "hell" in the Bible.

There are two other words that occasionally mean
something similar to hell. One is the word "Tartarus,"
which we find once in chapter 2 of Peter's second letter.
It's a term Peter borrowed from Greek mythology,
referring to the underworld, the place where the Greek
demigods were judged in the "abyss."

The other Greek word is "Hades."

Obscure, dark, murky—Hades is essentially the Greek
version of the Hebrew word "Sheol." We find the word
"Hades" in Revelation 1, 6, and 20 and in Acts 2, which is
a quote from Psalm 16. Jesus uses the word in Matthew
11 and Luke 10: "You will go down to Hades"; in Matthew
16: "The gates of Hades will not overcome it"; and in the
parable of the rich man and the beggar Lazarus in Luke 16.

And that's it.
Anything you have ever heard people say about the
actual word "hell" in the Bible they got from those verses
you just read.

For many in the modern world, the idea of hell is a
holdover from primitive, mythic religion that uses fear

and punishment to control people for all sorts of devious reasons. And so the logical conclusion is that we've evolved beyond all of that outdated belief, right?

I get that. I understand that aversion, and I as well have a hard time believing that somewhere down below the earth's crust is a really crafty figure in red tights holding a three-pointed spear, playing Pink Floyd records backward, and enjoying the hidden messages.

So how should we think,
or not think,
about hell?

I remember arriving in Kigali, Rwanda, in December 2002 and driving from the airport to our hotel. Soon after leaving the airport I saw a kid, probably ten or eleven, with a missing hand standing by the side of the road. Then I saw another kid, just down the street, missing a leg. Then another in a wheelchair. Hands, arms, legs—I must have seen fifty or more teenagers with missing limbs in just those first several miles. My guide explained that during the genocide one of the ways to most degrade and humiliate your enemy was to remove an arm or a leg of his young child with a machete, so that years later he would have to live with the reminder of what you did to him.

Do I believe in a literal hell?
Of course.
Those aren't metaphorical missing arms and legs.

Have you ever sat with a woman while she talked
about what it was like to be raped? How does a person
describe what it's like to hear a five-year-old boy whose
father has just committed suicide ask: "When is daddy
coming home?" How does a person describe that unique
look, that ravaged, empty stare you find in the eyes of a
cocaine addict?

I've seen what happens when people abandon all that is
good and right and kind and humane.

Once I conducted a funeral for a man I'd never met. His
children warned me when they asked me to do the service that I was getting into a mess and that the closer we
got to the service itself, the uglier it was going to get.

This man was cruel and mean. To everybody around
him. No one had anything positive to say about him. The
pastor's job, among other things, is to help family and
friends properly honor the dead. This man made my job
quite difficult.

I eventually realized what they meant by "ugly." When
he realized he was about to die, he had his will rewritten.
He purposely left relatives out who were expecting

something and gave that wealth to other family members he knew they despised. He had his will changed so that at his funeral there would be pain and anger. He wanted to make sure that he would be causing destruction in this life, even after he'd left it.

I tell these stories because it is absolutely vital that we acknowledge that love, grace, and humanity can be rejected. From the most subtle rolling of the eyes to the most violent degradation of another human, we are terrifyingly free to do as we please.

God gives us what we want, and if that's hell, we can have it.
We have that kind of freedom, that kind of choice. We are that free.

We can use machetes if we want to.

So when people say they don't believe in hell and they don't like the word "sin," my first response is to ask, "Have you sat and talked with a family who just found out their child has been molested? Repeatedly? Over a number of years? By a relative?"

Some words are strong for a reason. We need those words to be that intense, loaded, complex, and offensive, because they need to reflect the realities they describe.

And that's what we find in Jesus's teaching about hell—a volatile mixture of images, pictures, and metaphors that describe the very real experiences and consequences of rejecting our God-given goodness and humanity. Something we are all free to do, anytime, anywhere, with anyone.

He uses hyperbole often—telling people to gouge out their eyes and maim themselves rather than commit certain sins. It can all sound a bit over-the-top at times, leading us to question just what he's so worked up about. Other times he sounds just plain violent.

But when you've sat with a wife who has just found out that her husband has been cheating on her for years, and you realize what it is going to do to their marriage and children and finances and friendships and future, and you see the concentric rings of pain that are going to emanate from this one man's choices—in that moment Jesus's warnings don't seem that over-the-top or drastic; they seem perfectly spot-on.

Gouging out his eye may actually have been a better choice.

Some agony needs agonizing language.
Some destruction does make you think of fire.
Some betrayal actually feels like you've been burned.
Some injustices do cause things to heat up.

But it isn't just the striking images that stand out in Jesus's teaching about hell; it's the surreal nature of the stories he tells.

Jesus talks in Luke 16 about a rich man who ignored a poor beggar named Lazarus who was outside his gate. They both die, and the rich man goes to Hades, while Lazarus is "carried" by angels to "Abraham's side," a Jewish way of talking about what we would call heaven.

The rich man then asks Abraham to have Lazarus get him some water, because he is "in agony in this fire."

People in hell can communicate with people in bliss? The rich man is in the fire, and he can talk? He's surviving?

Abraham tells him it's not possible for Lazarus to bring him water. The rich man then asks that Lazarus be sent to warn his family of what's in store for them. Abraham tells him that's not necessary, because they already have that message in the scriptures. The man continues to plead with Abraham, insisting that if they could just hear from someone who came back from the dead, they would change their ways, to which Abraham replies, "If they do not listen to Moses and the prophets, they will not be convinced even if someone rises from the dead."

And that's the story.

Notice that the story ends with a reference to resurrection, something that was going to happen very soon with Jesus himself. This is crucial for understanding the story, because the story is about Jesus's listeners at that moment. The story, for them, moves from *then* to *now*. Whatever the meaning was for Jesus's first listeners, it was directly related to what he was doing right there in their midst.

Second, note what it is the man wants in hell: he wants Lazarus to get him water. When you get someone water, you're serving them.

The rich man wants Lazarus to serve him.

In their previous life, the rich man saw himself as better than Lazarus, and now, in hell, the rich man *still* sees himself as above Lazarus. It's no wonder Abraham says there's a chasm that can't be crossed. The chasm is the rich man's heart! It hasn't changed, even in death and torment and agony. He's still clinging to the old hierarchy. He still thinks he's better.

The gospel Jesus spreads in the book of Luke has as one of its main themes that Jesus brings a social revolution, in which the previous systems and hierarchies of clean and unclean, sinner and saved, and up and down don't mean what they used to. God is doing a new work through Jesus, calling all people to human solidarity. Everybody is a brother, a sister. Equals, children of the God who shows no favoritism.

To reject this new social order was to reject Jesus, the very movement of God in flesh and blood.

This story about the rich man and Lazarus was an incredibly sharp warning for Jesus's audience, particularly the religious leaders who Luke tells us were listening, to rethink how they viewed the world, because there would be serious consequences for ignoring the Lazaruses outside their gates. To reject those Lazaruses was to reject God.

What a brilliant, surreal, poignant, subversive, loaded story.

And there's more.

Jesus teaches again and again that the gospel is about a death that leads to life. It's a pattern, a truth, a reality that comes from losing your life and then finding it. This rich man Jesus tells us about hasn't yet figured that out. He's still clinging to his ego, his status, his pride—he's unable to let go of the world he's constructed, which puts him on the top and Lazarus on the bottom, the world in which *Lazarus* is serving *him*.

He's dead, but he hasn't died.

He's in Hades, but he still hasn't *died* the kind of death that actually brings life.

He's alive in death, but in profound torment, because he's living with the realities of not properly dying the kind of death that actually leads a person into the only kind of life that's worth living.

A pause, to recover from that last sentence.

How do you communicate a truth that complex and multilayered? You tell a nuanced, shocking story about a rich man and a poor man, and you throw in gruesome details about dogs licking his sores, and then you tell about a massive reversal in their deaths in which the rich man in hell has the ability to converse with Abraham, the father of the faith. And then you end it all with a twist about resurrection, a twist that is actually a hint about something about to happen in real history soon after this parable is told.

Brilliant, just brilliant.

There's more. The plot of the story spins around the heart of the rich man, who is a stand-in for Jesus's original audience. Jesus shows them the heart of the rich man, because he wants them to ask probing questions about their own hearts. It's a story about an individual, but how does the darkness of that individual's heart display itself?

He fails to love his neighbor.

In fact, he ignores his neighbor, who spends each day outside his gate begging for food, of which the rich man has plenty. It's a story about individual sin, but that individual sin leads directly to very real suffering at a societal level. If enough rich men treated enough Lazaruses outside their gates like that, that could conceivably lead to a widening gap between the rich and the poor.

Imagine.

Some people are primarily concerned with systemic evils—corporations, nations, and institutions that enslave people, exploit the earth, and disregard the welfare of the weak and disempowered. Others are primarily concerned with individual sins, and so they focus on personal morality, individual patterns, habits, and addictions that prevent human flourishing and cause profound suffering.

Some pass out pamphlets that explain how to have peace with God; some work in refugee camps in war zones. Some have radio shows that discuss particular interpretations of particular Bible verses; others work to liberate women and children from the sex trade.

Often the people most concerned about others going to hell when they die seem less concerned with the hells on earth right now, while the people most concerned with the hells on earth right now seem the least concerned about hell after death.

What we see in Jesus's story about the rich man and Lazarus is an affirmation that there are all kinds of hells, because there are all kinds of ways to resist and reject all that is good and true and beautiful and human now, in this life, and so we can only assume we can do the same in the next.

There are individual hells,
and communal, society-wide hells,
and Jesus teaches us to take both seriously.

There is hell now,
and there is hell later,
and Jesus teaches us to take both seriously.

So what about the passages in the Bible that don't specifically mention the word "hell," but clearly talk about judgment and punishment?

First, a political answer, then a religious answer, and then we'll look at a few of those passages.

Jesus lived in an incredibly volatile political climate. His native Israel had been conquered once again by another military superpower, this time the Roman Empire.

Roman soldiers were everywhere, patrolling the streets, standing guard over the temple in Jerusalem, reminding everybody of their conquest and power. There were a number of Jesus's contemporaries who believed that the only proper response to this outrage was to pick up swords and declare war.

Many in the crowds that followed Jesus assumed that he at some point would become one of those leaders, driving the Romans out of their land. But Jesus wasn't interested. He was trying to bring Israel back to its roots, to its divine calling to be a light to the world, showing the nations just what the redeeming love of God looks like. And he was confident that this love doesn't wield a sword. To respond to violence with more violence, according to Jesus, is not the way of God. We find him in his teachings again and again inviting his people to see their role in the world in a whole new way. As he says at one point, those who "draw the sword will die by the sword" (Matt. 26).

And so he rides into Jerusalem on a donkey, weeping because he realizes that they just don't get it. They're unable to see just what their insistence on violent revolt is going to cost them. He continually warns them how tragic the suffering will be if they actually try to fight Rome with the methods and mind-set of Rome.

When he warns of the "coming wrath," then, this is a very practical, political, heartfelt warning to his people to not go the way they're intent on going.

The Romans, he keeps insisting, will crush you.

The tragedy in all of this is that his warnings came true. In the great revolt that began in 66 CE, the Jews took up arms against the Romans—who eventually crushed them, grinding the stones of their temple into dust.

Because of this history, it's important that we don't take Jesus's very real and prescient warnings about judgment *then* out of context, making them about someday, somewhere else. That wasn't what he was talking about.

Now, a religious answer that begins with a question: Who is Jesus talking to? In general, in the Gospels and the stories about what he did, where he went, and what he said, who is he talking to most of the time?

Other than interactions with a Roman centurion and a woman by the well in Samaria and a few others, he's talking to very devoted, religious Jews. He's talking to people who saw themselves as God's people. Light of the world, salt of the earth, all that. His audience was people who were "in." Believers, redeemed, devoted, passionate, secure in their knowledge that they were God's chosen, saved, covenant people.

Many people in our world have only ever heard hell talked about as the place reserved for those who are "out," who don't believe, who haven't "joined the church." Christians talking about people who aren't Christians going to hell when they die because they aren't . . . Christians. People who don't believe the right things.

But in reading all of the passages in which Jesus uses the word "hell," what is so striking is that people believing the right or wrong things isn't his point. He's often not talking about "beliefs" as we think of them—he's talking about anger and lust and indifference. He's talking about the state of his listeners' hearts, about how they conduct themselves, how they interact with their neighbors, about the kind of effect they have on the world.

Jesus did not use hell to try and compel "heathens" and "pagans" to believe in God, so they wouldn't burn when they die. He talked about hell to very religious people to warn them about the consequences of straying from their God-given calling and identity to show the world God's love.

This is not to say that hell is not a pointed, urgent warning or that it isn't intimately connected with what we actually do believe, but simply to point out that Jesus talked about hell to the people who considered themselves "in," warning them that their hard hearts were putting their "in-ness" at risk, reminding them that whatever "chosen-ness" or "election" meant, whatever special standing they believed they had with God was always, only, ever about their being the kind of transformed, generous, loving people *through whom* God could show the world what God's love looks like in flesh and blood.

Now, on to the passages that seem to be talking about hell, but don't mention it specifically. Let's start with the story of Sodom and Gomorrah, the poster cities for deviant sinfulness run amok. In Genesis 19 we read that the city of Sodom has so lost its way, "the outcry to the LORD against its people is so great," that burning sulfur rains down from the heavens, "destroying all those living in the cities—and also the vegetation in the land."

"Early the next morning Abraham . . . looked down toward Sodom and Gomorrah . . . and he saw dense smoke rising from the land, like smoke from a furnace."

And so for thousands of years the words "Sodom and Gomorrah" have served as a warning, an ominous sign of just what happens when God decides to judge swiftly and decisively.

But this isn't the last we read of Sodom and Gomorrah.

The prophet Ezekiel had a series of visions in which God shows him what's coming, including the promise that God will "restore the fortunes of Sodom and her daughters" and they will "return to what they were before" (chap. 16).

Restore the fortunes of Sodom?
The story isn't over for Sodom and Gomorrah?

What appeared to be a final, *forever,* smoldering, smoking verdict regarding their destiny . . . wasn't?
What appeared to be over, isn't.
Ezekiel says that where there was destruction there will be restoration.

But that still isn't the last we hear of these two cities. As Jesus travels from village to village in Galilee, calling people to see things in a whole new way, he encounters great resistance in some areas, especially among the more religious and devout. In Matthew 10, he warns the people living in the village of Capernaum, "It will be more bearable for Sodom and Gomorrah on the day of judgment than for you."

More bearable for Sodom and Gomorrah?
He tells highly committed, pious, religious people that it will be better for Sodom and Gomorrah than them on judgment day?

There's still hope?

And if there's still hope for Sodom and Gomorrah,
what does that say about all of the other Sodoms and
Gomorrahs?

————————

This story, the one about Sodom and Gomorrah, isn't
the only place we find this movement from judgment to
restoration, from punishment to new life.

In Jeremiah 32, God says, "I will surely gather them from
all the lands where I banish them in my furious anger and
great wrath; I will bring them back to this place and let
them live in safety."

Israel had been exiled, sent away, "banished" to a foreign
land, the result of God's "furious anger and great wrath."
But there's a point to what the prophet interprets and
understands to be God's "anger and wrath." It's to teach
the people, to correct them, to produce something new
in them.

In Jeremiah 5, the prophet says, "You crushed them, but
they refused correction." That's the point, according to
the prophet, of the crushing. To bring about correction.

According to the prophets,
God crushes,
refines,
tests,
corrects,

chastens,
and rebukes—
but always with a purpose.

No matter how painful, brutal, oppressive, no matter
how far people find themselves from home because of
their sin, indifference, and rejection, there's always the
assurance that it won't be this way *forever.*

In Lamentations 3, the poet declares:
"People are not cast off by the Lord forever,
though he brings grief, he will show compassion,
so great is his unfailing love."

In Hosea 14 God says:
"I will heal their waywardness and love them freely
for my anger has turned away from them."

In chapter 3 Zephaniah says:
God "will take great delight in you;
in his love he will no longer rebuke you,
but will rejoice over you with singing."

No more anger, no more punishment, rebuke, or
refining—
at some point
healing
and reconciling
and return.

God promises in Isaiah 57: "I will guide them and restore
comfort to them."

In Hosea 6: "On the third day he will restore us, that we
may live in his presence."

In Joel 3: "In those days and at that time, when I restore
the fortunes of Judah and Jerusalem . . ."

In Amos 9: "I will restore David's fallen shelter."

In Nahum 2: "The LORD will restore the splendor of
Jacob."

In Zephaniah 2: "The LORD their God will care for them; he
will restore their fortunes."

In Zephaniah 3: "I will give you honor and praise among
all the peoples of the earth when I restore your fortunes
before your very eyes."

In Zechariah 9: "Even now I announce that I will restore
twice as much to you."

In Zechariah 10: "I will restore them because I have
compassion on them."

And in Micah 7: "You will again have compassion on us;
you will tread our sins underfoot and hurl all our iniquities
into the depths of the sea."

I realize that that's a lot of Bible verses, but I list them
to simply show how dominant a theme restoration is in
the Hebrew scriptures. It comes up again and again and
again. Sins trodden underfoot, iniquities hurled into the
depths of the sea. God always has an intention.

Healing.

Redemption.

Love.
Bringing people home and rejoicing over them with
singing.

The prophets are quick to point out that this isn't just
something for "God's people," the "chosen," the "elect."

In Isaiah 19, the prophet announces, "In that day there
will be an altar to the LORD in the heart of Egypt, and a
monument to the LORD at its border."

What's the significance of Egypt?

Egypt was Israel's enemy.
Hated.
Despised.
An altar in the heart of Egypt?
An altar was where people worshipped.
They'll worship God in . . . *Egypt*?

Once again, things aren't what they appear to be. The
people who are opposed to God will worship God, the
ones far away will be brought near, the ones facing
condemnation will be restored.

Failure, we see again and again, isn't final,
judgment has a point,
and consequences are for correction.

With this in mind, several bizarre passages later in the
New Testament begin to make more sense. In Paul's first
letter to Timothy he mentions Hymenaeus and Alexander,
whom he has "handed over to Satan to be taught not to
blaspheme." (Something in me wants to read that in a
Darth Vader voice.)

Now I realize that the moment he mentions Satan, things
can get really confusing. But beyond the questions—

"Handed over to Satan?"
Paul has handed people over to Satan?
Do you do that?
Can you do that?
How do you do that?
Is there paperwork involved?

What *is* clear is that Paul has great confidence that this
handing over will be for good, as inconceivable as that
appears at first. His confidence is that these two will be
taught something. They will learn. They will grow. They
will become better.

"Satan," according to Paul, is actually used by God for
God's transforming purposes. Whoever and whatever
he means by that word "Satan," there is something
redemptive and renewing that will occur when
Hymenaeus and Alexander are "handed over."

And this is not an isolated incident of Paul's confidence that the most severe judgment falls squarely within the redemptive purposes of God in the world. Paul gives a similar instruction in his first letter to the Corinthians, telling his friends to hand a certain man "over to Satan for the destruction of the sinful nature so that his spirit may be saved on the day of the Lord" (chap. 5).

How does that work? Because it's counterintuitive to say the least.

His assumption is that giving this man over to "Satan" will bring an end to the man's "sinful nature." It's as if Paul is saying, "We've tried everything to get his attention, and it isn't working, so turn him loose to experience the full consequences of his actions."

We have a term for this process. When people pursue a destructive course of action and they can't be convinced to change course, we say they're "hell-bent" on it. Fixed, obsessed, unshakable in their pursuit, unwavering in their commitment to a destructive direction. The stunning twist in all of this is that when God lets the Israelites go the way they're insisting on heading and when Paul "turns people over," it's all for good. The point of this turning loose, this letting go, this punishment, is to allow them to live with the full consequences of their choices, confident that the misery they find themselves in will have a way of getting their attention.

As God says time and time again in the Prophets, "I've tried everything else, and they won't listen." The result, Paul is convinced, is that wrongdoers will become right doers.

We see this same impulse in the story Jesus tells in Matthew 25 about sheep and goats being judged and separated. The sheep are sent to one place, while the goats go to another place because of their failure to see Jesus in the hungry and thirsty and naked.

The goats are sent, in the Greek language, to an *aion* of *kolazo*. *Aion,* we know, has several meanings. One is "age" or "period of time"; another refers to intensity of experience. The word *kolazo* is a term from horticulture. It refers to the pruning and trimming of the branches of a plant so it can flourish.

An *aion* of *kolazo*. Depending on how you translate *aion* and *kolazo*, then, the phrase can mean "a period of pruning" or "a time of trimming," or an intense experience of correction.

In a good number of English translations of the Bible, the phrase "*aion* of *kolazo*" gets translated as "eternal punishment," which many read to mean "punishment forever," as in never going to end.

But "forever" is not really a category the biblical writers used.

The closest the Hebrew writers come to a word for "forever" is the word *olam*. *Olam* can be translated as "to the vanishing point," "in the far distance," "a long time," "long lasting," or "that which is at or beyond the horizon." When *olam* refers to God, as in Psalm 90 ("from everlasting to everlasting you are God"), it's much closer to the word "forever" as we think of it, time without beginning or end. But then in the other passages, when it's not describing God, it has very different meanings, as when Jonah prays to God, who let him go down into the belly of a fish "forever" (*olam*) and then, three days later, brought him out of the belly of the fish.

Olam, in this instance,
turns out to be three days.

It's a versatile, pliable word,
in most occurrences referring to a particular period of time.

So when we read "eternal punishment," it's important that we don't read categories and concepts into a phrase that aren't there. Jesus isn't talking about forever as we think of forever. Jesus may be talking about something else, which has all sorts of implications for our understandings of what happens after we die, which we'll spend the next chapter sorting through.

_____

To summarize, then, we need a loaded, volatile, adequately violent, dramatic, serious word to describe the very real consequences we experience when we reject the good and true and beautiful life that God has for us. We need a word that refers to the big, wide, terrible evil that comes from the secrets hidden deep within our hearts all the way to the massive, society-wide collapse and chaos that comes when we fail to live in God's world God's way.

And for that,
the word "hell" works quite well.
Let's keep it.

CHAPTER 4

DOES GOD GET WHAT GOD WANTS?

On the websites of many churches, there is a page where you can read what the people in that particular church believe. Usually the list starts with statements about the Bible, then God, Jesus, and the Spirit, then salvation and the church, and so on. Most of these lists and statements include a section on what the people in the church believe about the people who don't believe what they believe.

This is from an actual church website: "The unsaved will be separated forever from God in hell."

This is from another: "Those who don't believe in Jesus will be sent to eternal punishment in hell."

And this is from another: "The unsaved dead will be committed to an eternal conscious punishment."

So in the first statement, the "unsaved" won't be with God.
In the second, not only will they not be with God, but they'll be sent somewhere else to be punished.
And in the third, we're told that not only will these "unsaved" be punished forever, but they will be fully aware of it—in case we were concerned they might down an Ambien or two when God wasn't looking . . .

The people experiencing this separation and punishment will feel all of it, we are told, because they'll be fully conscious of it, fully awake and aware for every single second of it, as it never lets up for billions and billions of years.

All this,
on a website.

Welcome to our church.

Yet on these very same websites are extensive affirmations of the goodness and greatness of God, proclamations and statements of belief about a God who is
"mighty,"
"powerful,"

"loving,"
"unchanging,"
"sovereign,"
"full of grace and mercy,"
and "all-knowing."

This God is the one who created
"the world and everything in it."

This is the God for whom
"all things are possible."

I point out these parallel claims:
that God is mighty, powerful, and "in control"
and that billions of people will spend forever apart from
this God, who is their creator,
even though it's written in the Bible that
"God wants all people to be saved and to come to a
knowledge of the truth" (1 Tim. 2).

So does God get what God wants?

How great is God?
Great enough to achieve what God sets out to do,
or kind of great,
medium great,
great most of the time,
but in this,
the fate of billions of people,

not totally great.

Sort of great.

A little great.

According to the writer of the letter to the Hebrews, "God wanted to make the unchanging nature of his purpose very clear" (chap. 6).

God has a purpose, something God is doing in the world, something that has never changed, something that involves everybody, and God's intention all along has been to communicate this intention clearly.

Will all people be saved, or will God not get what God wants?

Does this magnificent, mighty, marvelous God *fail* in the end?

People, according to the scriptures, are inextricably intertwined with God. As it's written in Psalm 24: "The earth is the Lord's, and everything in it, the world, and all who live in it."

The prophet Isaiah, in chapter 45, says that God "did not create [the earth] to be empty, but formed it to be inhabited." Paul says in a speech in Acts 17 that in God "we live and move and have our being," and he writes in Romans 11, "From him and through him and to him are all things."

The prophet Malachi asks, "Do we not all have one Father? Did not one God create us?" (chap. 2). Paul says in Acts 17, "We are God's offspring," and in Ephesians 3 he writes, "I kneel before the Father, from whom every family in heaven and on earth derives it name."

The writers of the scriptures consistently affirm that we're all part of the same family. What we have in common—regardless of our tribe, language, customs, beliefs, or religion—outweighs our differences. This is why God wants "all people to be saved." History is about the kind of love a parent has for a child, the kind of love that pursues, searches, creates, connects, and bonds. The kind of love that moves toward, embraces, and always works to be reconciled with, regardless of the cost.

The writers of the Bible have a lot to say about this love: In Psalm 65 it's written that "all people will come" to God. In Ezekiel 36 God says, "The nations will know that I am the Lord."
The prophet Isaiah says, "All the ends of the earth will see the salvation of our God" (chap. 52).
Zephaniah quotes God as saying, "Then I will purify the lips of the peoples, that all of them may call on the name of the Lord and serve him shoulder to shoulder" (chap. 3).
And Paul writes in Philippians 2, "Every knee should bow . . . and every tongue acknowledge that Jesus Christ is Lord, to the glory of God the Father."

All people.
The nations.
Every person, every knee, every tongue.

Psalm 22 echoes these promises: "All the ends of the earth will remember and turn to the Lord, and all the families of the nations will bow down before him."

But then it adds a number of details:
"All the rich of the earth will feast and worship;
all who go down to the dust will kneel before him—"

So everybody who dies will kneel before God, and "future generations will be told about the Lord. They will proclaim his righteousness, declaring to a people yet unborn: He has done it!"

This insistence that God will be united and reconciled with all people is a theme the writers and prophets return to again and again. They are very specific in their beliefs about who God is and what God is doing in the world, constantly affirming the simple fact that God does not fail.

In the book of Job the question arises: "Who can oppose God? He does whatever he pleases" (chap. 23). And then later it's affirmed when Job says to God, "I know that you can do all things; no purpose of yours can be thwarted" (chap. 42).

Through Isaiah God says, "I will do all that I please." Isaiah asks, "Surely the arm of the LORD is not too short to save, nor his ear too dull to hear?" while Jeremiah declares to God, "Nothing is too hard for you" (Isa. 46; 59; Jer. 32).

This God, in Psalm 145, "is good to all; he has compassion on all he has made."
This God's anger, in Psalm 30, "lasts only a moment, but his favor lasts a lifetime."
This God, in Psalm 145, "is gracious and compassionate, slow to anger and rich in love."

In the Bible, God is not helpless,
God is not powerless,
and God is not impotent.

Paul writes to the Philippians that "it is God who works in you to will and to act in order to fulfill his good purpose" (chap. 2).

Once again, God has a purpose. A desire. A goal. And God never stops pursuing it. Jesus tells a series of parables in Luke 15 about a woman who loses a coin, a shepherd who loses a sheep, and a father who loses a son. The stories aren't ultimately about things and people being lost; the stories are about things and people being found. The God that Jesus teaches us about doesn't give up until everything that was lost is found. This God simply doesn't give up. Ever.

Now, back to those church websites, the ones that declare that ultimately billions of people will spend eternity apart from God, while others will be with God in heaven forever.

Is history tragic?
Have billions of people been created only to spend eternity in conscious punishment and torment, suffering infinitely for the finite sins they committed in the few years they spent on earth?
Is our future uncertain,
or will God take care of us?
Are we safe?
Are we secure?
Or are we on our own?

Is God our friend, our provider, our protector, our father—
or is God the kind of judge who may in the end declare that we deserve to spend forever separated from our Father?
Is God like the characters in a story Jesus would tell, old ladies who keep searching for the lost coin until they find it,
shepherds who don't rest until that one sheep is back in the fold,
fathers who rush out to greet and embrace their returning son,
or, in the end, will God give up?

Will "all the ends of the earth" come, as God has decided,
or only some?
Will all feast as it's promised in Psalm 22,
or only a few?
Will everybody be given a new heart,
or only a limited number of people?
Will God, in the end, settle, saying:
"Well, I tried, I gave it my best shot,
and sometimes you just have to be okay with failure"?
Will God shrug God-size shoulders and say,
"You can't always get what you want"?

Now, on to some specific responses.

There are those, like the church websites quoted at the
beginning of this chapter, who put it quite clearly: "We
get one life to choose heaven or hell, and once we die,
that's it. One or the other, forever."

God in the end doesn't get what God wants, it's declared,
because some will turn, repent, and believe, and others
won't. To explain this perspective, it's rightly pointed
out that love, by its very nature, is freedom. For there
to be love, there has to be the option, both now and
then, to not love. To turn the other way. To reject the
love extended. To say no. Although God is powerful and
mighty, when it comes to the human heart God has to
play by the same rules we do. God has to respect our
freedom to choose to the very end, even at the risk of the

relationship itself. If at any point God overrides, co-opts, or hijacks the human heart, robbing us of our freedom to choose, then God has violated the fundamental essence of what love even is.

The question that flows out of this understanding of love, then, is quite simple. Lots of people in our world right now choose to be violent and abusive and mean and evil, so why won't they continue to choose this path after they die?

That question leads to another idea, one rooted in the dynamic nature of life. We aren't fixed, static beings—we change and morph as life unfolds. As we choose evil, it often leads to more evil. Tell a lie, and moments later you find yourself telling another lie to cover up the first lie. And so on.

When we choose to reject our God-given humanity, we can easily find ourselves in a rut, wearing grooves in a familiar path that is easier and easier to take. One lie leads to another, one act of violence demands another, and on and on it goes, gaining momentum all the while. This is how addiction works: something gets its claws into us and, as it becomes more and more dominant in our life, it becomes harder and harder to imagine living without it.

What makes us think that after a lifetime, let alone hundreds or even thousands of years, somebody who has consciously chosen a particular path away from God suddenly wakes up one day and decides to head in the completely opposite direction?

And so a universal hugfest where everybody eventually ends up around the heavenly campfire singing "Kumbaya," with Jesus playing guitar, sounds a lot like fantasy to some people.

Although we're only scratching the surface of this perspective—the one that says we get this life and only this life to believe in Jesus—it is safe to say that this perspective is widely held and passionately defended by many in our world today.

Others hold this perspective (that there is this lifetime and only this lifetime in which we all choose one of two possible futures), but they suggest a possibility involving the image of God in each of us. We can nurture and cultivate this divine image, or we can ignore, deny, and stifle it. If we can do this now, becoming less and less humane in our treatment of ourselves and others, what would happen if this went on unchecked for years and years? Would a person's humanity just ebb away eventually? Could a person reach the point of no longer bearing the image of God? Could the divine image be extinguished in a person, given enough time and neglect? Is there a possibility that, given enough time, some people could eventually move into a new state, one in which they were in essence "formerly human" or "posthuman" or even "ex-human?"

An interesting question.

And then there are others who can live with two destinations, two realities after death, but insist that there must be some kind of "second chance" for those who don't believe in Jesus in this lifetime. In a letter Martin Luther, one of the leaders of the Protestant Reformation, wrote to Hans von Rechenberg in 1522 about the possibility that people could turn to God after death, asking: "Who would doubt God's ability to do that?"

Again, a good question.

And so space is created in this "who would doubt God's ability to do that?" perspective for all kinds of people—fifteen-year-old atheists, people from other religions, and people who rejected Jesus because the only Jesus they ever saw was an oppressive figure who did anything but show God's love.

And then there are others who ask, if you get another chance after you die, why limit that chance to a one-off immediately after death? And so they expand the possibilities, trusting that there will be endless opportunities in an endless amount of time for people to say yes to God.

As long as it takes, in other words.

At the heart of this perspective is the belief that, given enough time, everybody will turn to God and find themselves in the joy and peace of God's presence. The love of God will melt every hard heart, and even the most "depraved sinners" will eventually give up their resistance and turn to God.

And so, beginning with the early church, there is a long tradition of Christians who believe that God will ultimately restore everything and everybody, because Jesus says in Matthew 19 that there will be a "renewal of all things," Peter says in Acts 3 that Jesus will "restore everything," and Paul says in Colossians 1 that through Christ "God was pleased to . . . reconcile to himself all things, whether things on earth or things in heaven."

In the third century the church fathers Clement of Alexandria and Origen affirmed God's reconciliation with all people.
In the fourth century, Gregory of Nyssa and Eusebius believed this as well.
In their day, Jerome claimed that "most people," Basil said the "mass of men," and Augustine acknowledged

that "very many" believed in the ultimate reconciliation of all people to God.

Central to their trust that all would be reconciled was the belief that untold masses of people suffering forever doesn't bring God glory. Restoration brings God glory; eternal torment doesn't. Reconciliation brings God glory; endless anguish doesn't. Renewal and return cause God's greatness to shine through the universe; never-ending punishment doesn't.

To be clear, again, an untold number of serious disciples of Jesus across hundreds of years have assumed, affirmed, and trusted that no one can resist God's pursuit forever, because God's love will eventually melt even the hardest of hearts.

Could God say to someone truly humbled, broken, and desperate for reconciliation, "Sorry, too late"? Many have refused to accept the scenario in which somebody is pounding on the door, apologizing, repenting, and asking God to be let in, only to hear God say through the keyhole: "Door's locked. Sorry. If you had been here earlier, I could have done something. But now, it's too late."

As it's written in 2 Timothy 2, God "cannot disown himself."

As Abraham asked in Genesis 18, "Will not the Judge of all the earth do right?"

Which is stronger and more powerful, the hardness of the human heart or God's unrelenting, infinite, expansive love? Thousands through the years have answered that question with the resounding response, "God's love, of course."

As John reminds his church in his first letter, "The one who is in you is greater than the one who is in the world" (chap. 4); and Paul declares in 1 Corinthians 13, "Love never fails."

At the center of the Christian tradition since the first church have been a number who insist that history is not tragic, hell is not forever, and love, in the end, wins and all will be reconciled to God.

To reflect on these perspectives we've briefly covered, two observations and then a picture from the end of the Bible.

First, an obvious but unfortunately much needed observation: People have answered these questions about who goes where, when, why, and how in a number of ways. Or, to be more specific, serious, orthodox followers of Jesus have answered these questions in a number of different ways. Or, to say it another way, however you answer these questions, there's a good chance you can find a Christian or group of Christians somewhere who would answer in a similar way.

It is, after all, a wide stream we're swimming in.

Many people find Jesus compelling, but don't follow him, because of the parts about "hell and torment and all that." Somewhere along the way they were taught that the only option when it comes to Christian faith is to clearly declare that a few, committed Christians will "go to heaven" when they die and everyone else will not, the matter is settled at death, and that's it. One place or the other, no looking back, no chance for a change of heart, make your bed now and lie in it . . . forever.

Not all Christians have believed this, and you don't have to believe it to be a Christian. The Christian faith is big enough, wide enough, and generous enough to handle that vast a range of perspectives.

Second, it's important that we be honest about the fact that some stories are better than others. Telling a story in which billions of people spend forever somewhere in the universe trapped in a black hole of endless torment and misery with no way out isn't a very good story. Telling a story about a God who inflicts unrelenting punishment on people because they didn't do or say or believe the correct things in a brief window of time called life isn't a very good story.

In contrast, everybody enjoying God's good world together with no disgrace or shame, justice being served, and all the wrongs being made right is a better story. It is bigger, more loving, more expansive, more extraordinary, beautiful, and inspiring than any other story about the ultimate course history takes.

Whatever objections a person might have to this story, and there are many, one has to admit that it is fitting, proper, and Christian to long for it. We can be honest about the warped nature of the human heart, the freedom that love requires, and the destructive choices people make, and still envision God's love to be bigger, stronger, and more compelling than all of that put together. To shun, censor, or ostracize someone for holding this belief is to fail to extend grace to each other in a discussion that has had plenty of room for varied perspectives for hundreds of years now.

Now, on to a picture we're given in the last few chapters of the Bible.

The last book in the Bible is the Book of Revelation, a complex, enigmatic letter from a pastor named John filled with scenes of scrolls and robes and angels and plagues and trumpets and horses and dragons and beasts and bowls and prostitutes and horses.

Women sit on scarlet beasts,
swords come out of mouths,

and in a "lake of fire" death and Hades experience a "second death."

This letter is written in an apocalyptic, heavily symbolic way that has given people much to discuss over the years, beginning with the question: How did the first readers of this letter understand it? Because it's written by a real pastor in a real place to a real congregation going through very real suffering. They were living at the time the letter was written under the oppressive rule of a succession of Roman Emperors who demanded they be worshipped as the "Son of God." Christians who refused to acknowledge these Caesars as Lord were being executed, simply for being followers of Jesus.

This kind of tribulation raised very pressing questions for these people in this church that John pastored about how God runs the world and how long God would let this injustice continue. And so, at the heart of the letter he paints a picture for them of God acting decisively to restrain evil and conquer all who trample on the innocent and the good. In the end, wrongs are righted and people are held accountable for the destruction they have caused.

But the letter does not end with blood and violence.

It ends with two chapters describing a new city, a new creation, a new world that God makes, right here in the midst of this one. It is a buoyant, hopeful vision of a future in which the nations are healed and there is peace on earth and there are no more tears.

This vision we're given here in the final words of the Bible tells us all kinds of things about the big story, the one Jesus invites us in to, the one rooted in, driven by and permeated with God's love.

First, we read that there is no place in this new world for murder and destruction and deceit. There can't be because this new world is free from those evils, which means that it is free from those who would insist on continuing to perpetuate those evils.

This is important, because in speaking of the expansive, extraordinary, infinite love of God there is always the danger of neglecting the very real consequences of God's love, namely God's desire and intention to see things become everything they were always intended to be. For this to unfold, God must say about a number of acts and to those who would continue to do them, "Not here you won't."

Love demands freedom. It always has, and it always will. We are free to resist, reject, and rebel against God's ways for us. We can have all the hell we want.

Let's pause here and ask the obvious question: How could someone choose another way with a universe of love and joy and peace right in front of them—all of it theirs if they would simply leave behind the old ways and receive the new life of the new city in the new world?

The answer to how is "Yes."

I see this every day, and so do you. People choose to live in their own hells all the time. We do it every time we isolate ourselves, give the cold shoulder to someone who has slighted us, every time we hide knives in our words, every time we harden our hearts in defiance of what we know to be the loving, good, and right thing to do.

Have you ever been in an argument and you knew exactly what not to say? You knew exactly what would most wound the person, what would unnecessarily drag the past up, what would get right to the person's heart in the quickest, most hurtful way—and yet you said that very thing anyway? Me, too.

We see people choose another way all the time. That impulse lurks in all of us. So will those who have said no to God's love in this life continue to say no in the next? Love demands freedom, and freedom provides that possibility. People take that option now, and we can assume it will be taken in the future.

Second, we read in these last chapters of Revelation that the gates of that city in that new world will "never shut." That's a small detail, and it's important we don't get too hung up on details and specific images because it's

possible to treat something so literally that it becomes
less true in the process. But gates, gates are for keeping
people in and keeping people out. If the gates are never
shut, then people are free to come and go.

Can God bring proper, lasting justice, banishing certain
actions—and the people who do them—from the new
creation while at the same time allowing and waiting and
hoping for the possibility of the reconciliation of those
very same people? Keeping the gates, in essence, open?
Will everyone eventually be reconciled to God or will
there be those who cling to their version of their story,
insisting on their right to be their own little god ruling
their own little miserable kingdom?

Will everybody be saved,
or will some perish apart from God forever because of
their choices?

Those are questions, or more accurately, those are
tensions we are free to leave fully intact. We don't need
to resolve them or answer them because we can't, and so
we simply respect them, creating space for the freedom
that love requires.

This space leads to a third observation about the new
creation in this new city in the world we see at the end
of Revelation: God announces "I am making everything
new." At the end, something new. The last word, it turns
out, isn't a last word but a first word. Or more precisely,

another first word in an endless succession of first words. That's what God's love does: it speaks new words into the world and into us. Potentials, possibilities, and the promise that God has an imagination and is not afraid to use it. Hard and fast, definitive declarations then, about how God will or will not organize the new world must leave plenty of room for all kinds of those possibilities. This doesn't diminish God's justice or take less seriously the very real consequences of sin and rebellion, it simply acknowledges with humility the limits of our powers of speculation.

Now back to that original question: "Does God get what God wants?" is a good question, an interesting question, an important question that gives us much to discuss.

But there's a better question, one we can answer, one that takes all of this speculation about the future, which no one has been to and then returned with hard, empirical evidence, and brings it back to one absolute we can depend on in the midst of all of this, which turns out to be another question.
It's not "Does God get what God wants?"
but
"Do we get what we want?"

And the answer to that is a resounding, affirming, sure, and positive yes.
Yes, we get what we want.

God is that loving.

If we want isolation, despair, and the right to be our own god, God graciously grants us that option. If we insist on using our God-given power and strength to make the world in our own image, God allows us that freedom; we have the kind of license to that. If we want nothing to do with light, hope, love, grace, and peace, God respects that desire on our part, and we are given a life free from any of those realities. The more we want nothing to do with all God is, the more distance and space are created. If we want nothing to do with love, we are given a reality free from love.

If, however, we crave light,
we're drawn to truth,
we're desperate for grace,
we've come to the end of our plots and schemes
and we want someone else's path,
God gives us what we want.

If we have this sense
that we've wandered far from home,
and we want to return,
God is there,
standing in the driveway,
arms open,
ready to invite us in.

If we thirst for *shalom,*

and we long for the peace that transcends
all understanding,
God doesn't just give,
they're poured out on us,
lavished,
heaped,
until we're overwhelmed.
It's like a feast where the food and wine do not run out.

These desires can start with the planting of an infinitesimally small seed deep in our heart, or a yearning for life to be better, or a gnawing sense that we're missing out, or an awareness that beyond the routine and grind of life there's something more, or the quiet hunch that this isn't all there is. It often has its birth in the most unexpected ways, arising out of our need for something we know we do not have, for someone we know we are not.

And to that,
that impulse, craving, yearning, longing, desire—
God says yes.
Yes, there is water for that thirst,
food for that hunger,
light for that darkness,
relief for that burden.
If we want hell,
if we want heaven,
they are ours.

That's how love works. It can't be forced, manipulated, or coerced.
It always leaves room for the other to decide.
God says yes,
we can have what we want,
because love wins.

CHAPTER 5

DYING TO LIVE

Somewhere around 2005 Eminem dropped out of sight. No albums, no tours—not much was heard from him. Word spread that he'd been battling a drug addiction, and many wondered if he'd ever come back. And then in the summer of 2010, he announced that he'd be doing a concert in his hometown of Detroit. A comeback, if there ever was one.

I remember standing there among forty thousand people in that baseball stadium when he first took the stage and his image was projected onto the massive screens on the sides of the stage. It was then that I noticed something fascinating.

Eminem was wearing a cross around his neck.

Now, we see crosses all the time, that's nothing new.

They're around somebody's neck,
on a church building,
on a sign at a sporting event.
It's an icon,
a sign,
a sculpture,
it's on someone's arm as a tattoo—
the cross is everywhere.

Companies and institutions spend millions of dollars to
come up with logos that we will notice, remember, and
associate with certain products, people, or ideas. But
this one, hundreds of years after its inception, this simple
icon with its two intersecting sticks, has endured in a way
very few images ever have.

But this ubiquity is dangerous, because it can inoculate.
Familiarity can lead to unfamiliarity. We see something
so much that we assume we know and understand what
it is.

"Jesus died on the cross for your sins."
Yes, we know. We've seen that homemade billboard by
the side of the road countless times.
Anything else?

Yes, there is.

———————

First, a question. How often do you slit the throat of a
goat?

(Didn't see that coming, did you?)

Now another one. Do you regularly head downtown to a
temple, maybe on a Saturday night, to sprinkle yourself
with the blood of a bull?

And then one more. Do you ever strangle a bird and then
place it on an altar for good luck?

It's been a while, hasn't it?

Because you don't. Ever. Just the thought of such
practices and rituals is repulsive. So primitive and
barbaric. Not to mention unnecessary. It doesn't even
cross our minds to sacrifice animals.

Exactly.

We read in Hebrews 9 that Jesus "has appeared once for
all at the culmination of the ages to do away with sin by
the sacrifice of himself."

In the ancient world, people regularly sacrificed animals—
bulls, goats, sheep, birds. You raised or purchased
an animal and then brought it to the temple and said
the right words at the right time. Then the animal was
slaughtered, and its blood shed on an altar to show the

gods that you were very sorry for any wrong you'd done and you were very grateful for the rain and crops and children and any other gifts you could think of that the gods had given you.

Entire civilizations for thousands of years enacted sacrificial rituals, because people believed that this was how you maintained a peaceful relationship with the gods, the forces, and the deities who controlled your fate.

You wanted whoever controlled the sun and rain to be on your side.
You wanted whoever dictated whether a woman got pregnant to show you favor.
You wanted the one who decides who wins or loses in battle to decide that you should be victorious.

That's how it worked. Offer something, show that you're serious, make amends, find favor, and then hope that was enough to get what you needed.

So when the writer of Hebrews insisted that Jesus was the last sacrifice ever needed, that was a revolutionary idea. To make that claim in those days? Stunning. Unprecedented.

Whole cultures centered around keeping the gods pleased. This was obviously a very costly, time-consuming ordeal, not to mention an anxiety-producing one. You never knew if you'd fully pleased the gods and paid the debt properly. And now the writer is announcing that those days are over because of Jesus dying on the cross. Done away with. Gone. Irrelevant.

The psychological impact alone would have been extraordinary—no more anxiety, no more worry, no more stress, no more wondering if the gods were pleased with you or ready to strike you down. There was no more need for any of that sacrifice, because Jesus was the ultimate sacrifice that thoroughly pleased the only God who ever mattered.

That's how the writer of Hebrews explains what happened when Jesus died on the cross.

Perhaps you've heard all of this before.
Excellent.
Because there's more.

In a different book in the New Testament, Paul writes to the Colossians that through the cross God was reconciling "to himself all things, whether things on earth or things in heaven, by making peace through his blood, shed on the cross" (chap. 1). "Reconciliation" is a word from the world of relationships. It's what happens when two people or groups have had something come between them, some argument or difference or wrong or injustice, and now they've found a way to work it out and come back together. Peace has been made.

They've been reconciled.

Paul takes something we experience in relationships and says, essentially, "That's what happened on the cross." God has made peace with "all things."

So when Jesus died on the cross,
was it the end of the sacrificial system
or was it the reconciling of all things?

Which was it?

But then in Romans 3, Paul writes that we've been justified by grace through faith in Jesus. "Justified" is a legal term, from the world of courtrooms and judges and prosecutors and guilt and punishment. Paul talks about our world as if it's a courtroom and we're guilty, standing before the judge, with no hope. Jesus, Paul says, paid the price for our sins, so that we could go free.

Again, which is it?
When Jesus died on the cross,
was it the end of sacrifices
or the reconciling of all things
or the price paid to free guilty sinners?

But then Paul writes in 2 Timothy 1 that Jesus has "destroyed death," and John writes in chapter 5 of his first letter that "this is the victory that has overcome the world." "Victory" and "destroyed" are terms from battle—they're war metaphors from the world of armies and soldiers and conquest. In these texts, the cross is explained in terms of Jesus's winning a battle against evil.

And then, in the first chapter of his letter to the Ephesians, Paul writes, "We have redemption through his blood." "Redemption" is a word from the world of business and finance and economics. To redeem something is to give it worth again, to revalue it, to buy it back.

So, back to the question: What happened on the cross?

Is the cross about the end of the sacrificial system
or a broken relationship that's been reconciled
or a guilty defendant who's been set free
or a battle that's been won
or the redeeming of something that was lost?

Which is it?

Which perspective is the right one? Which metaphor is correct? Which explanation is true?

The answer, of course, is yes.

So why all the different explanations?

For these first Christians, something massive and universe-changing had happened through the cross, and they set out to communicate the significance and power of it to their audiences in language their audiences would understand. And so they looked at the world around them, identifying examples, pictures, experiences, and metaphors that their listeners and readers would have already been familiar with, and then they essentially said:

What happened on the cross is like . . .

a defendant going free,
a relationship being reconciled,
something lost being redeemed,
a battle being won,
a final sacrifice being offered,
so that no one ever has to offer another one again,
an enemy being loved.

For the first thousand years or so of church history, the metaphor of victory in battle, Jesus conquering death, was the central, dominant understanding of the cross. And then at other times and in other places, other explanations have been more heavily emphasized.

This is especially crucial in light of how many continue to use the sacrificial metaphor in our modern world. There's nothing wrong with talking and singing about how the "Blood will never lose its power" and "Nothing but the blood will save us." Those are powerful metaphors. But we don't live any longer in a culture in which people offer animal sacrifices to the gods. People did live that way for thousands of years, and there are pockets of primitive cultures around the world that do continue to understand sin, guilt, and atonement in those ways. But most of us don't. What the first Christians did was look around them and put the Jesus story in language their listeners would understand.

"It's like this . . ."
"It's like that . . ."

The point, then, isn't to narrow it to one particular metaphor, image, explanation, or mechanism. To elevate one over the others, to insist that there's a "correct" or "right" one, is to miss the brilliant, creative work these first Christians were doing when they used these images and metaphors. They were reading their world, looking for ways to communicate this epic event in ways their listeners could grasp.

The point then, as it is now, is Jesus. The divine in flesh and blood. He's where the life is.

———————

So far, we've just explored the cross.
So now, the resurrection.
Because after Friday eventually comes . . . Sunday.

Lots of people were crucified in Jesus's day. That wasn't that unusual. What gave the early Christians such extraordinary fire and fuel was the insistence that

Jesus's death on the cross was not the last word on this rabbi from Nazareth. What set all sorts of historic events in motion was his followers' insistence that they had experienced him *after his death.* Their encounters with him led them to believe that something massive had happened that had implications for the entire world.

To understand their claims, it's important to remember that resurrection after death was not a new idea. In the fall in many parts of the world, the leaves drop from the trees and the plants die. They turn brown, wither, and lose their life. They remain this way for the winter—dormant, dead, lifeless. And then spring comes, and they burst into life again. Growing, sprouting, producing new leaves and buds. For there to be spring, there has to be a fall and then a winter. For nature to spring to life, it first has to die. Death, then resurrection. This is true for ecosystems, food chains, the seasons—it's true all across the environment. Death gives way to life.

A seed has to be buried in the ground before it can rise up from out of the earth as new life.

Think of what you've had to eat today.

Dead. All of it. If you ate plants, they were at some point harvested, uprooted, disconnected from a stalk or vine, yanked from the ground so that they could make their

way to your plate, where you ate them so that you can . . .
live. The death of one living thing for the life of another.

This death-and-life mystery, this mechanism, this process
is built into the very fabric of creation. The cells in our
bodies are dying at a rate of millions a second, only to
be replaced at a similar rate of millions a second. Our
skin is constantly flaking off and our body is continually
replacing the skin cells with new ones; we have entirely
new skin every week or so.

Death is the engine of life in the relational realm as well.
Think about those firefighters who lost their lives on 9/11
rescuing people. Who isn't moved when they hear those
stories of selfless heroism? We talk about how inspiring it
is when people sacrifice themselves for the well-being of
another. To inspire is to give life. Their deaths for others'
lives.

So when the writers of the Bible talk about Jesus's
resurrection bringing new life to the world, they aren't
talking about a new concept. They're talking about
something that has always been true. It's how the world
works.

Although the cross is often understood as a religious
icon, it's a symbol of an elemental reality, one we all
experience every time we take a bite of food.

Once again, death and rebirth are as old as the world.

Second, then, these first Christians understood the cross and resurrection to be an event as wide as the world, extending to all of creation.

Here's an example from early in John's Gospel. John tells a story about Jesus turning water into wine at a wedding (chap. 2) and then mentions that this was the first "sign" Jesus performed. Then, two chapters later, Jesus heals an official's son, and John mentions that this was "the second sign Jesus performed."

Why does John number the signs?

One of the things you pick up in reading the Bible over time is that the writers were extremely clever, employing incredibly complex patterns with numbers and hints and allusions in their writings. Often just below the surface they would place another story, another point.

So when John numbers these first two signs, we are wise to begin asking questions. Why the numbers? What's he getting at? If we then read on, looking for more signs, we see Jesus heal a man by a pool in the next chapter. That would be the third sign in the Gospel. Then in chapter 6 he provides bread for the crowd and then walks on water. Those would be signs four and five. Then in chapter 9 he heals a blind man, which would be sign six. And then, in chapter 11, he raises Lazarus from the dead, a "sign" if there ever was one.

Seven signs.

Now ask: Is the number seven significant in the Bible? Does it occur in any other prominent place?

Well, yes, it does. In the poem that begins the Bible. The poem speaks of seven days of creation.

But there's one more sign in John's Gospel. In chapter 20 Jesus rises from the dead. Now *that's* a sign. The eighth sign in the book of John. Jesus rises from the dead in a garden. Which, of course, takes us back to Genesis, to the first creation in a . . . garden.

What is John telling us?
It's the eighth sign, the first day of the new week, the first day of the new creation. The resurrection of Jesus inaugurates a new creation, one free from death, and it is bursting forth in Jesus himself right here in the midst of the first creation.

The tomb is empty,
a new day is here,
a new creation is here,
everything has changed,
death has been conquered,

the old has gone,
the new has come.

John is telling a huge story,
one about God rescuing all of creation.

When people say that Jesus came to die on the cross so
that we can have a relationship with God, yes, that is true.
But that explanation as the first explanation puts *us* at
the center. For the first Christians, the story was, first and
foremost, bigger, grander. More massive. When Jesus
is presented only as the answer that saves individuals
from their sin and death, we run the risk of shrinking the
Gospel down to something just for humans, when God
has inaugurated a movement in Jesus's resurrection to
renew, restore, and reconcile everything "on earth or in
heaven" (Col. 1), just as God originally intended it. The
powers of death and destruction have been defeated
on the most epic scale imaginable. Individuals are then
invited to see their story in the context of a far larger
story, one that includes all of creation.

Yes, it includes people. The writers were very clear
that the good news of the cross and resurrection is
for everybody. Paul writes in 1 Corinthians 15 that all of
humanity died through the first humans, so "in Christ
all will be made alive." He writes to Titus that "the grace
of God has appeared that offers salvation to all people"
(chap. 2). And then, in one of his more epic passages,
Paul explains to the Romans that "just as one trespass

resulted in condemnation for all people, so also one righteous act resulted in justification and life for all" (chap. 5).

He is not alone in this belief. The pastor John writes to his people that Jesus is "the Lamb of God, who takes away the sin of the world" and that Jesus is "the atoning sacrifice for our sins, and not only for ours but also for the sins of the whole world" (John 1; 1 John 2).

How many people, if you were to ask them why they've left church, would give an answer something along the lines of, "It's just so . . . small"?

Of course.
A gospel that leaves out its cosmic scope will always feel small.
A gospel that has as its chief message avoiding hell or not sinning will never be the full story.
A gospel that repeatedly, narrowly affirms and bolsters the "in-ness" of one group at the expense of the "out-ness" of another group will not be true to the story that includes "all things and people in heaven and on earth."

And then, third, the cross and resurrection are personal. This cosmic event has everything to do with how every single one of us lives every single day. It is a pattern, a rhythm, a practice, a reality rooted in the elemental realities of creation, extending to the very vitality of our soul.

When we say yes to God, when we open ourselves to Jesus's living, giving act on the cross, we enter in to a way of life. He is the source, the strength, the example, and the assurance that this pattern of death and rebirth is the way into the only kind of life that actually sustains and inspires.

Jesus talks about death and rebirth constantly, his and ours. He calls us to let go, turn away, renounce, confess, repent, and leave behind the old ways. He talks of the life that will come from his own death, and he promises that life will flow to us in thousands of small ways as we die to our egos, our pride, our need to be right, our self-sufficiency, our rebellion, and our stubborn insistence that we deserve to get our way. When we cling with white knuckles to our sins and our hostility, we're like a tree that won't let its leaves go. There can't be a spring if we're still stuck in the fall.

Lose your life and find it, he says.
That's how the world works.
That how the soul works.
That's how life works when you're dying to live.

————————

Did Eminem stumble upon this truth?
Did he, somewhere in his addiction and despair and pain, hit bottom hard enough that something died—the old,

the hard, that which could never bring life in the first
place?

Did he stumble into that truth that's as old as the
universe—
that life comes through death?
Did he in some strange way die,
and that's why he's back?

Is that why he wore a cross around his neck?
Because we all want new life.
We want to know that the last word hasn't been spoken,
we want to know that the universe is on our side,
we want to know on Friday that Sunday will eventually
come.

That is why the cross continues to endure.
It's a reminder, a sign, a glimpse, an icon that allows us
to tap into our deepest longings to be part of a new
creation.

Because that's how the universe works.
That's what Jesus does.
Death and resurrection.
Old life for new life;
one passes away, the other comes.
Friday, then Sunday.
You die, and you're reborn.
It's like that.

CHAPTER 6

THERE ARE ROCKS EVERYWHERE

About a year into my first job as a pastor, I met a man who told me that he used to stay up all night every night, smoking pot and drawing at his kitchen table until going to bed at dawn. On one of those nights just like any other he was all alone in his kitchen smoking his usual pot and drawing his usual drawings, when he became aware of the kitchen filling with an overwhelming presence of warmth and love. The power of this presence was so strong and forceful that he was unable to remain in his chair. Struck to the ground, lying prostrate on the kitchen floor in the middle of the night, he said that he knew without a doubt in that moment that it was God telling him that he is loved absolutely and unconditionally and that the only possible path for his life was to receive that love and become a follower of Jesus.

Which he did.

And his life was never the same again.

Now, there are some who hear a story like this and say, "Isn't it great how God works?" There are others, of a more mystical bent, who smile in a Zen-like way and say, "Well, the spirit does move in mysterious ways . . ." And then there are others, like me, whose first thought upon hearing a story like this one is:

"Must have been *some* weed."

And then there are still others who would point out that the story is crazy and highlights how religion naturally draws the unstable, odd, and weak-minded among us, who claim to have experiences that then support their pathologies and dysfunction.

You turn the light on, you get all kinds of bugs.

The problem with his story, though, is that I've heard countless stories like it. Bizarre, strange, weird— unexplainable. And yet real.

For every one I dismiss, I hear ten that can't be as easily denied. Even in their kooky oddness they contain something strangely true.

Several years after hearing that story, I went to the hospital to visit a man who had survived a terrible accident at work. He'd been repairing the ceiling of a massive warehouse, high up off the floor on a lift that had tipped, pinning him against one of the support beams. He was essentially crushed between the lift and the beam, with his feet dangling there, a hundred or so feet off the ground.

He told me that as he blacked out he saw a white light.

(Doesn't everybody? Come on, at least make up some details we haven't heard a thousand times!)

He said that he knew instantly that the white light was powerfully good and right, but it produced in him a profound sense that he wasn't that good and right. That there were things in him that the light revealed, things he didn't want revealed, and so he kept repeating, as fast as he could get the words out, as if he couldn't help it, "Please forgive me, please forgive me, please forgive me, please forgive me," and then

he came to,
in the hospital.

What kind of universe are we living in?
Is it safe or dangerous?
Is there a force, an energy, a being calling out to us,
in many languages, using a variety of methods and events,
trying to get our attention?

Or are we alone in the world?
Should we dismiss those experiences that come out of
nowhere,
the love that creeps in, with no explanation, at the
strangest times,
the quiet grace that grabs hold of us in the middle of the
night and assures us that we're going to be fine?

And what does any of this have to do with Jesus?

To answer that,
another odd story.

This one is an old one, from early in the Bible, Exodus
17. Moses and the Israelites have left Egypt, and they're
traveling from "place to place as the LORD commanded."

It's not going well. The Israelites are thirsty, they can't
find water, and they're angry with Moses, demanding to
know why he brought them out of Egypt only to make
them and their children and livestock "die of thirst."
Moses cries out to God, "What am I to do with these
people?"

God tells him to strike a rock with his staff in front of all
the people.

He does,
and out of the rock comes . . .
water.

What an odd story.
What an odd rock.

The story goes on, telling us about their continuing journey, the obstacles in their way, God's patience with them, and Moses learning how hard it is to lead people and not lose your sanity in the process.

But the rock—we don't hear any more about the rock.

Until more than a thousand years later.

In a letter to the Corinthians, the apostle Paul refers to this story about this rock, saying that those who traveled out of Egypt "drank from the spiritual rock that accompanied them, and that rock was Christ" (1 Cor. 10).

That rock was . . . Christ? Jesus?

Jesus was the rock?

How is that? Christ is mentioned nowhere in the story. Moses strikes the rock, it provides water, and the people have something to drink.

Story over.

Paul, however, reads another story in the story, insisting that Christ was present in that moment, that Christ was providing the water they needed to survive—that Jesus was giving, quenching, sustaining.

Jesus was, he says, the rock.

According to Paul,
Jesus was there.
Without anybody using his name.
Without anybody saying that it was him.
Without anybody acknowledging just what—or, more
precisely, who—it was.

Paul's interpretation that Christ was present in the
Exodus raises the question:
Where else has Christ been present?
When else?
With who else?
How else?

Paul finds Jesus there,
in that rock,
because Paul finds Jesus everywhere.

To understand why, it's important to understand how the
first Christians thought about the world.

———————

There is an energy in the world, a spark, an electricity
that everything is plugged into. The Greeks called it *zoe*,
the mystics call it "Spirit," and Obi-Wan called it "the
Force."

How does the sun give off that much energy and yet still regenerate itself at the same time?

How do bees know to take that pollen from that flower over there and put it over here in this one?

Why does my lawn have brown patches where I can't get the grass to grow, while five feet away grass grows through the cracks in the concrete in the driveway, grass much like the grass I wish would grow in those brown patches?

This energy, spark, and electricity that pulses through all of creation sustains it, fuels it, and keeps it going. Growing, evolving, reproducing, making more.

In many traditions, this energy is understood to be impersonal. Much like the Force in *Star Wars,* it has no name or face or personality. It's assumed to be indifferent to us. Our joy, meaning, and happiness are simply irrelevant. It does its thing; we do ours.

This is not, however, how things are explained in the creation poem that begins the Bible. In this poem, the energy that gives life to everything is called the "Word of God," and it is *for* us.

God speaks . . . and it happens.
God says it . . . and it comes into being.

Before, it's chaotic and empty and dark. But then God speaks into that dark disorder radiant, pulsating life with all of its wonder and diversity and creativity.

Order out of chaos.
Life and light out of darkness and emptiness.

Here's where the claims of the first Christians come in. They believed that at a specific moment in the history of the world, that life-giving "Word of God" took on flesh and blood. In Jesus, they affirmed, was that word, that *divine* life-giving energy that brought the universe into existence. The word that gave life to everything and continues to give life to everything, they insisted, had been revealed "in its fullness."

John begins his Gospel by claiming that through Jesus "all things were made." It's written in Hebrews 1 that Jesus is the one "through whom also [God] made the universe"; in Colossians 1, "He is before all things"; in Ephesians 4 he's "the very one who ascended higher than all the heavens, in order to fill the whole universe"; and in 1 Corinthians 8 he's "Jesus Christ," the one "through whom all things came and through whom we live."

This is an astounding claim, and one that causes many to get off the bus at the nearest stop. Too out there, too mythic, premodern, or superstitious to be taken seriously in our modern world. Haven't we evolved past such nonsense? God became a man?

It's a common protest, and it's understandable.
It is, at the same time, unavoidable.
It's the heart of the Jesus story.

If you find yourself checking out at this point, finding it hard to swallow the Jesus-as-divine part, remember that these are ultimately issues that ask what kind of universe we believe we're living in. Is it closed or open? Is it limited to what we can conceive of and understand, or are there realities beyond the human mind? Are we the ultimate orbiter of what can, and cannot, exist?

Or is the universe open, wondrous, unexpected, and far beyond anything we can comprehend?

Are you open or closed?

The insistence of the first Christians was that when you saw Jesus—the first-century Jewish rabbi who taught and healed and called disciples and challenged the authorities to the point of death—you were seeing the divine in skin and bones, the *word* in flesh and blood.

Jesus, then, wasn't a new idea.

Jesus wasn't something God cooked up at the last minute to try to rescue us from what happened when we were given the freedom to truly make a mess of things.

Jesus, for these first Christians, was the ultimate exposing of what God has been up to all along.

This is, of course, a mystery,
which is exactly the word they used for it.

In Ephesians 1, Paul writes that it's a mystery "God has made known to us . . . according to his good pleasure."

What a great word there, "pleasure." This mystery begins with God's pleasure. And this pleasure comes from God's purpose, which is "to bring unity to all things in heaven and on earth under Christ."

Unity.
To all things.
God is putting the world back together,
and God is doing this through Jesus.

In Colossians 1, Paul writes, "God has chosen to make known among the Gentiles the glorious riches of this mystery."

This use of the word "Gentiles" is significant, because for many of Paul's Jewish tribe, whatever God was doing in the world God was doing through, and for, them.

Their tribe,
their people,
their faith.

The ones who believed and lived like them.

Us, not them.
We, not you.

But Paul's insistence here is that what God is doing in Christ is for everybody, every nation, every ethnic group, every tribe. Paul uses the expansive word "Gentiles"—a first-century way of saying "everybody else."

Something hidden that is now being revealed.
Something God has been up to all along that is now being made known.

It's a mystery that Paul, in Romans 11, doesn't want us to be "ignorant of," and in Colossians 2, his desire is that people "may have the full riches of complete understanding, in order that they may know the mystery of God."

Now, Paul is very clear that this mystery has existed from before the very beginning of everything. He writes, in Romans 16, of "the revelation of the mystery hidden for the long ages past, but now revealed and made known," while in Ephesians 3 he writes of "the mystery of Christ, which was not made known to people in other generations as it has now been revealed."

There is a mystery,
something hidden in God,
something that has existed
and been true and been present with, and in, God since before time,
and that mystery is a someone . . .
Christ.
Jesus.

As obvious as it is, then, Jesus is bigger than any one religion.

He didn't come to start a new religion, and he continually disrupted whatever conventions or systems or establishments that existed in his day. He will always transcend whatever cages and labels are created to contain and name him, especially the one called "Christianity."

Within this proper, larger understanding of just what the Jesus story even is, we see that Jesus himself, again and again, demonstrates how seriously he takes his role in saving and rescuing and redeeming not just everything, but everybody.

He says in John 12, "And I, when I am lifted up from the earth, will draw all people to myself."

He is sure, confident, and set on this.
All people, to himself.

In John 6, speaking of his own life, his own body, he says, "This bread is my flesh, which I will give for the life of the world."

He takes this very personally.
He is willing to die for this,
"for the life of the world."

Jesus is supracultural.
He is present within all cultures,
and yet outside of all cultures.

He is for all people,
and yet he refuses to be co-opted or owned by any one culture.

That includes any Christian culture. Any denomination. Any church. Any theological system. We can point to him, name him, follow him, discuss him, honor him, and believe in him—but we cannot claim him to be ours any more than he's anyone else's.

Access to him can actually function in a strangely inverse way.

Imagine a high-school student whose family is part of a Christian church. She belongs to a Christian youth group, has only Christian friends, reads only Christian books and has to attend Christian chapel services, because it's mandatory at the Christian high school she attends.

That student can potentially become so anesthetized to Jesus that she in unable to see Jesus as the stunning, dangerous, compelling, subversive, dynamic reality that he is. She has simply sung so many songs about Jesus that the name has lost its power to provoke and inspire.

Her "nearness" can actually produce distance.

At the same time, there are Christians who have raised support, gathered supplies, traveled thousands of miles into the farthest reaches of the globe to share the good news of Jesus with "unreached people," who upon hearing of Jesus for the "first time," respond, "That's his name? We've been talking about him for years . . ."

As Jesus says in John 10, "I have other sheep that are not of this sheep pen."

This should not surprise us. The gospel, Paul writes in his letter to the Colossians, "has been proclaimed to every creature under heaven" (chap. 1).

Every.
Creature.
Under.
Heaven.

As wide as creation.
Including everybody.
The whole world.

This is crucial for how we understand the current state of world religions, with its staggering number of religions themselves, let alone the multitudes of splinter groups and subgroups and denominations and factions and varied interpretations.

Religions should not surprise us. We crave meaning and order and explanation. We're desperate for connection with something or somebody greater than ourselves. This is not new. This has not caught Jesus off guard. Jesus insisted in the midst of this massive array of belief and practice that God was doing something new in human history, something through him, something that involved everybody.

John remembers Jesus saying, "I am the way and the truth and the life. No one comes to the Father except through me" (chap. 14).

This is as wide and expansive a claim as a person can make.

What he doesn't say is how, or when, or in what manner the mechanism functions that gets people to God through him. He doesn't even state that those coming to the Father through him will even know that they are coming exclusively through him. He simply claims that whatever God is doing in the world to know and redeem and love and restore the world is happening through him.

And so the passage is exclusive, deeply so, insisting on Jesus alone as the way to God. But it is an exclusivity on the other side on inclusivity.

First, there is exclusivity.
Jesus is the only way. Everybody who doesn't believe in him and follow him in the precise way that is defined by the group doing the defining isn't saved, redeemed, going to heaven, and so on. There is that kind of exclusion. You're either in, or you're going to hell. Two groups.

Then there is inclusivity.
The kind that is open to all religions, the kind that trusts that good people will get in, that there is only one

mountain, but it has many paths. This inclusivity assumes that as long as your heart is fine or your actions measure up, you'll be okay.

And then there is an exclusivity on the other side of inclusivity. This kind insists that Jesus is the way, but holds tightly to the assumption that the all-embracing, saving love of this particular Jesus the Christ will of course include all sorts of unexpected people from across the cultural spectrum.

As soon as the door is opened to Muslims, Hindus, Buddhists, and Baptists from Cleveland, many Christians become very uneasy, saying that then Jesus doesn't matter anymore, the cross is irrelevant, it doesn't matter what you believe, and so forth.

Not true.
Absolutely, unequivocally, unalterably not true.

What Jesus does is declare that he,
and he alone,
is saving everybody.

And then he leaves the door way, way open. Creating all sorts of possibilities. He is as narrow as himself and as wide as the universe.

He is as exclusive as himself and as inclusive as containing every single particle of creation.

When people use the word "Jesus," then, it's important for us to ask who they're talking about.

Are they referring to a token of tribal membership, a tamed, domesticated Jesus who waves the flag and promotes whatever values they have decided their nation needs to return to?
Are they referring to the supposed source of the imperial impulse of their group, which wants to conquer other groups "in the name of Jesus"?
Are they referring to the logo or slogan of their political, economic, or military system through which they sanctify their greed and lust for power?

Or are they referring to the very life source of the universe who has walked among us and continues to sustain everything with his love and power and grace and energy?

Jesus is both near and intimate and personal, and big and wide and transcendent.

One of the many things people in a church do, then, is name, honor, and orient themselves around this mystery. A church is a community of people who enact specific rituals and create specific experiences to keep this word alive in their own hearts, a gathering of believers who help provide language and symbols and experiences for this mystery.

When we baptize, we lower people into the water,
and then bring them back up out of the water.
The water signifies death;
being raised up out of it signifies life.
Lowered like Christ in his death,
raised like Christ in his life.

When we take the Eucharist, or Communion,
we dip bread into a cup,
enacting and remembering Jesus's gift of himself.
His body,
his blood,
for the life of the world.
Our bodies, our lives,
for the life of the world.

These rituals are true for us,
because they're true for everybody.
They unite us, because they unite everybody.

These are signs, glimpses, and tastes of what is true
for all people in all places at all times—we simply name
the mystery present in all the world, the gospel already
announced to every creature under heaven.

He holds the entire universe in his embrace.
He is within and without time.
He is the flesh-and-blood exposure of an eternal reality.

He is the sacred power present in every dimension of creation.

———————

So how does any of this explanation of who Jesus is and what he's doing connect with heaven, hell, and the fate of every single person who has ever lived?

First, we aren't surprised when people stumble upon this mystery, whenever and however that happens. We aren't offended when they don't use the exact language we use, and we aren't surprised when their encounters profoundly affect them, even if they happen way outside the walls of our particular Jesus's gathering.

People come to Jesus in all sorts of ways.

Sometimes people bump into Jesus,
they trip on the mystery,
they stumble past the word,
they drink from the rock,
without knowing what or who it was.
This happened in the Exodus,
and it happens today.
The last thing we should do is discourage or disregard
an honest, authentic encounter with the living Christ.
He is the rock, and there is water for the thirsty there,
wherever *there* is.

We are not threatened by this,
surprised by this,
or offended by this.

Sometimes people use his name;
other times they don't.

Some people have so much baggage with regard to the
name "Jesus" that when they encounter the mystery
present in all of creation—grace, peace, love, acceptance,
healing, forgiveness—the last thing they are inclined to
name it is "Jesus."

Second, none of us have cornered the market on Jesus,
and none of us ever will.

What we see Jesus doing again and again—in the midst
of constant reminders about the seriousness of following
him, living like him, and trusting him—is widening the
scope and expanse of his saving work.

His disciples want to shut down a man healing in his
name in Luke 9, but he says sharply, "Do not stop him,
for whoever is not against you is for you." He praises the
faith of a Roman centurion, a "sinful woman" wastes a ton
of money on perfume and he calls it worship, and when
he encounters a despised tax collector, he wants to have
dinner with him.

Whatever categories have been created, whatever biases are hanging like a mist in the air, whatever labels and assumptions have gone unchecked and untested, he continually defies, destroys, and disregards.

Third, it is our responsibility to be extremely careful about making negative, decisive, lasting judgments about people's eternal destinies. As Jesus says, he "did not come to judge the world, but to save the world" (John 12). We can name Jesus, orient our lives around him, and celebrate him as the way, the truth, and the life, and at the same time respect the vast, expansive, generous mystery that he is.

Heaven is, after all, full of surprises.

This world is being redeemed,
the tomb is empty,
and a new creation is bursting forth
right here in the midst of this one.

Jesus said in Matthew 13 that this new reality is like yeast, working its way slowly and quietly, and steadily, through the dough. In the story he tells in Matthew 25, the mystery hides in the naked and hungry and sick and lonely. And in another parable he tells, also in Matthew 13, the kingdom is like a mustard seed that grows and grows and grows until it's a massive tree.

Not everybody sees it,
not everybody recognizes it,
but everybody is sustained by it.

He is the answer,
but he is also the question,
the hunt,
the search,
the exploration,
the discovery.

He is the rock,
and there is water there.

CHAPTER 7

THE GOOD NEWS IS BETTER THAN THAT

On the Sundays when I give a sermon at our church, I usually sit on the edge of the stage and talk to people after the service. And every week the same woman walks up to me and hands me a piece of paper. We've been going through this ritual for several years now. She smiles, and we chat for a moment or two, and then she walks away. The piece of paper she hands me is always the same size, about four by five inches, folded, with writing inside in the upper left corner. I unfold it each week while she watches, and then I read what she's written on it.

A number, with a few comments next to the number.

Sometimes the number is big, like 174.

Sometimes it's smaller. I remember once when it was 2.

The number is how many days it's been since she last cut herself. She's struggled with a self-injury addiction for years, but lately a group of people have been helping her find peace and healing. But she still struggles, some weeks more than others.

She recently told me that every man she's ever been with hit her.

So when she hears about love,
it's not a concept she's familiar with.

Which makes sense.

Beaten, hit, abused, neglected—and then she's told that God loves her unconditionally without reservation without her having to do anything to earn it?

That's a stretch. Hard to believe, given what she's seen of the world.

I tell you a bit of her story in order to tell another story, one Jesus tells in Luke 15. A man has two sons. The younger one demands his share of the father's inheritance early, and the father unexpectedly gives it to him. He takes the money, leaves home, spends it all, and returns home hoping to be hired as a worker in his dad's business. His father, again unexpectedly, welcomes him home, embraces him, and throws him a homecoming party, fattened calf and all.

Which his older brother refuses to join. It's unfair, he tells his father, because he's never even been given a goat, so that he and his friends could have a party. The father then says to him, "You are always with me, and everything I have is yours. But we had to celebrate and be glad, because this brother of yours was dead and is alive again; he was lost and is found."

I retell this story of Jesus's, because of the number of stories being told in this one story.

The younger brother tells a story. It is his version of his story, and as he heads home in shame after squandering his father's money, he rehearses the speech he'll give his father. He is convinced he's "no longer worthy" to be called his father's son. That's the story he's telling, that's the one he's believing. It's stunning, then, when he gets home and his father demands that the best robe be put on him and a ring placed on his finger and sandals on his feet. Robes and rings and sandals are signs of being a son. Although he's decided he can't be a son anymore, his father tells a different story. One about return and reconciliation and redemption. One about his being a son again.

The younger son has to decide whose version of his story he's going to trust: his or his father's. One in which he is no longer worthy to be called a son or one in which he's a robe-, ring-, and sandal-wearing son who was dead but is alive again, who was lost but has now been found.

There are two versions of his story.
His.
And his father's.

He has to choose which one he will live in.
Which one he will believe.
Which one he will trust.

Same, it turns out, for the older brother.
He too has his version of his story.
He tells his father, "All these years I've been slaving for you and never disobeyed your orders. Yet you never gave me even a young goat so I could celebrate with my friends. But when this son of yours

(he can't even say his brother's name)

who has squandered your property with prostitutes comes home, you kill the fattened calf for him!"

So much in so few words. One senses he's been saving it up for years, and now out it comes, with venom.

First, in his version of events, he's been slaving for his father for years. That's how he describes life in his father's house: slaving. That directly contradicts the few details we've been given about the father, who appears to be anything but a slave driver.

Second, he says his father has never even given him a goat. A goat doesn't have much meat on it, so even in conjuring up an image of celebration, it's meager. Lean. Lame. The kind of party he envisions just isn't that impressive. What he reveals here is what he really thinks about his father: he thinks he's cheap.

Third, he claims that his father has dealt with his brother according to a totally different set of standards. He thinks his father is unfair. He thinks he's been wronged, shorted, shafted. And he's furious about it.

All with the party in full swing in the background.

The father isn't rattled or provoked. He simply responds, "My son, you are always with me, and everything I have is yours." And then he tells him that they have to celebrate.

"You are always with me,
and everything I have is yours."

In one sentence the father manages to tell an entirely different story about the older brother.

First, the older son hasn't been a slave. He's had it all the whole time. There's been no need to work, obey orders, or slave away to earn what he's had the whole time.

Second, the father hasn't been cheap with him. He could have had whatever he wanted whenever he wanted it. Everything the father owns has always been his, which includes, of course, fattened calves. All he had to do was receive.

Third, the father redefines fairness. It's not that his father hasn't been fair with him; it's that his father never set out to be fair in the first place. Grace and generosity aren't fair; that's their very essence. The father sees the younger brother's return as one more occasion to practice *unfairness*. The younger son doesn't deserve a party—that's the point of the party. That's how things work in the father's world. Profound unfairness.

People get what they don't deserve.
Parties are thrown for younger brothers who squander their inheritance.

After all,
"You are always with me,
and everything I have is yours."

What the father does is retell the older brother's story. Just as he did with the younger brother. The question, then, is the same question that confronted the younger

brother—will he trust his version of his story or his
father's version of his story?

Who will he trust?
What will he believe?

The difference between the two stories is,
after all,
the difference between heaven . . . and hell.

Now most images and understandings people have of
heaven and hell are conceived of in terms of separation.

Heaven is "up" there,
hell is "down" there.

Two different places,
far apart from each other.

One over *there,*
the other over *there.*

This makes what Jesus does in his story about the man
with two sons particularly compelling. Jesus puts the
older brother right there at the party, but refusing to
trust the father's version of his story. Refusing to join in
the celebration.

Hell is being at the party.
That's what makes it so hellish.

It's not an image of separation,
but one of integration.

In this story, heaven and hell are within each other,
intertwined, interwoven, bumping up against each other.

If the older brother were off, alone in a distant field,
sulking and whining about how he's been a slave all these
years and never even had a goat to party with his friends
with, he would be alone in his hell.
But in the story Jesus tells, he's at the party, with the
music in the background and the celebration going on
right there in front of him.

There is much for us here,
about heaven,
hell,
and the news that is good.

First, an observation about hell.

Hell is our refusal to trust God's retelling of our story.

We all have our version of events. Who we are, who we
aren't, what we've done, what that means for our future.
Our worth, value, significance. The things we believe

about ourselves that we cling to despite the pain and agony they're causing us.

Some people are haunted by the sins of the past. Abuse, betrayal, addiction, infidelity—secrets that have been buried for years. I can't tell you how many people I've met over the years who said they couldn't go to a church service, because the "roof would cave in" or "there would be a lightning bolt."

Flaws, failures, shame like a stain that won't wash out. A deep-seated, profound belief that they are, at some primal level of the soul, not good enough.

For others, it isn't their acute sense of their lack or inadequacy or sins; it's their pride. Their ego. They're convinced of their own greatness and autonomy—they don't need anybody. Often the belief is that God, Jesus, church, and all that is for the "weak ones," the ones who can't make it in the world, so they cling to religious superstitions and myths like a drug, a crutch, a way to avoid taking responsibility for their pathetic lives.

We believe all sorts of things about ourselves.

What the gospel does is confront our version of our story with God's version of our story.

It is a brutally honest,
exuberantly liberating story,
and it is good news.

It begins with the sure and certain truth that we are
loved.
That in spite of whatever has gone horribly wrong deep
in our hearts
and has spread to every corner of the world,
in spite of our sins,
failures,
rebellion,
and hard hearts,
in spite of what's been done to us or what we've done,
God has made peace with us.

Done. Complete.
As Jesus said, "It is finished."

We are now invited to live a whole new life without guilt
or shame or blame or anxiety. We are going to be fine. Of
all of the conceptions of the divine, of all of the language
Jesus could put on the lips of the God character in this
story he tells, that's what he has the father say.

"You are always with me, and everything I have is yours."

The older brother has been clinging to his version of
events for so long, it's hard for him to conceive of any
other way of seeing things.

And so the father's words, which are generous and loving, are also difficult and shocking.

Again, then, we create hell whenever we fail to trust God's retelling of our story.

The older brother's failure to trust, we learn, is rooted in his distorted view of God. There is a problem with his "God."

This story, the one Jesus tells about the man with two sons, has everything to do with our story. Millions of people in our world were told that God so loved the world, that God sent his Son to save the world, and that if they accept and believe in Jesus, then they'll be able to have a relationship with God.

Beautiful.

But there's more. Millions have been taught that if they don't believe, if they don't accept in the right way, that is, the way the person telling them the gospel does, and they were hit by a car and died later that same day, God would have no choice but to punish them forever in conscious torment in hell. God would, in essence, become a fundamentally different being to them in that moment of death, a different being to them *forever.* A loving heavenly father who will go to extraordinary lengths to have a relationship with them would, in the blink of an eye, become a cruel, mean, vicious tormenter

who would ensure that they had no escape from an
endless future of agony.

If there was an earthly father who was like that, we would
call the authorities.
If there was an actual human dad who was that volatile,
we would contact child protection services immediately.

If God can switch gears like that, switch entire modes
of being that quickly, that raises a thousand questions
about whether a being like this could ever be trusted, let
alone be good.

Loving one moment, vicious the next.
Kind and compassionate, only to become cruel and
relentless in the blink of an eye.

Does God become somebody totally different the
moment you die?

That kind of God is simply devastating.
Psychologically crushing.
We can't bear it.
No one can.

And that is the secret deep in the heart of many people,
especially Christians: they don't love God. They can't,
because the God they've been presented with and

taught about can't be loved. That God is terrifying and traumatizing and unbearable.

And so there are conferences about how churches can be more "relevant" and "missional" and "welcoming," and there are vast resources, many, many books and films, for those who want to "reach out" and "connect" and "build relationships" with people who aren't part of the church. And that can be helpful. But at the heart of it, we have to ask: Just what kind of God is behind all this?

Because if something is wrong with your God,
if your God is loving one second and cruel the next,
if your God will punish people for all of eternity for sins committed in a few short years,
no amount of clever marketing
or compelling language
or good music
or great coffee
will be able to disguise
that one, true, glaring, untenable, unacceptable, awful reality.

Hell is refusing to trust, and refusing to trust is often rooted in a distorted view of God. Sometimes the reason people have a problem accepting "the gospel" is that they sense that the God lurking behind Jesus isn't safe, loving, or good. It doesn't make sense, it can't be reconciled, and so they say no. They don't want anything to do with Jesus, because they don't want anything to do with that God.

What we see in the older brother is that our beliefs matter. They are incredibly important. Our beliefs shape us and guide us and determine our lives.

We can trust God's retelling of our story,
or we can cling to our version of our story.
And to trust God's telling,
we have to trust God.

Several distinctions are important here.
First, one about our choices. We are free to accept or reject the invitation to new life that God extends to us. Our choice.

We're at the party,
but we don't have to join in.
Heaven or hell.
Both at the party.

There are consequences for the older brother,
just as there are for us.

To reject God's grace,
to turn from God's love,
to resist God's telling,
will lead to misery.
It is a form of punishment, all on its own.

This is an important distinction, because in talking about what God is like, we cannot avoid the realities of God's very essence, which is love. It can be resisted and rejected and denied and avoided, and that will bring another reality. Now, and then.

We are that free.

When people say they're tired of hearing about "sin" and "judgment" and "condemnation," it's often because those have been confused for them with the nature of God. God has no desire to inflict pain or agony on anyone.

God extends an invitation to us, and we are free to do with it is as we please.

Saying yes will take us in one direction; saying no will take us in another.

God is love, and to refuse this love moves us away from it, in the other direction, and that will, by very definition, be an increasingly unloving, hellish reality.

We do ourselves great harm when we confuse the very essence of God, which is love, with the very real consequences of rejecting and resisting that love, which creates what we call hell.

Second, another distinction to be clear about,
one between entrance and enjoyment.

God is love,
And love *is* a relationship.
This relationship is one of joy, and it can't be contained.

Like when you see something amazing and you turn
to those you're with and say, "Isn't this great?" Your
question is an invitation for them to join you in your joy.
The amazement you are experiencing can't be contained;
it spills over the top; it compels you to draw others into it.
You have to share it.

God creates, because the endless joy and peace and
shared life at the heart of this God knows no other way.

Jesus invites us into *that* relationship, the one at the
center of the universe. He insists that he's one with God,
that we can be one with him, and that life is a generous,
abundant reality. This God whom Jesus spoke of has
always been looking for partners, people who are
passionate about participating in the ongoing creation of
the world.

So when the gospel is diminished to a question of
whether or not a person will "get into heaven," that
reduces the good news to a ticket, a way to get past the
bouncer and into the club.

The good news is better than that.

This is why Christians who talk the most about going to heaven while everybody else goes to hell don't throw very good parties.

When the gospel is understood primarily in terms of entrance rather than joyous participation, it can actually serve to cut people off from the explosive, liberating experience of the God who is an endless giving circle of joy and creativity.

Life has never been about just "getting in." It's about thriving in God's good world. It's stillness, peace, and that feeling of your soul being at rest, while at the same time it's about asking things, learning things, creating things, and sharing it all with others who are finding the same kind of joy in the same good world.

Jesus calls disciples to keep entering into this shared life of peace and joy as it transforms our hearts, until it's the most natural way to live that we can imagine. Until it's second nature. Until we naturally embody and practice the kind of attitudes and actions that will go on in the age to come. A discussion about how to "just get into heaven" has no place in the life of a disciple of Jesus, because it's missing the point of it all.

An entrance understanding of the gospel rarely creates good art. Or innovation. Or a number of other things. It's a cheap view of the world, because it's a cheap view of God. It's a shriveled imagination.

It's the gospel of goats.

It's bound up in fear and scarcity, so people are left having to explain why others seem to be having so much fun and actually enjoying life while they aren't. This can be especially true in missionary settings or in pastors' families or in church communities where people have picked up along the way the toxic notion that God is a slave driver. A quiet resentment can creep in that comes from believing that they're sacrificing so much *for God,* while others get off easy. Hell can easily become a way to explain all of this: "Those people out there may be going to parties and appearing to have fun while the rest of us do 'God's work,' but someday we'll go to heaven, where *we won't have to do anything,* and they'll go to hell, where *they'll get theirs.*"

I have sat with many Christian leaders over the years who are burned out, washed up, fried, whose marriages are barely hanging on, whose kids are home while the parents are out at church meetings, who haven't taken a vacation in forever—all because, like the older brother, they have seen themselves as "slaving all these years." They believe that they believe the right things and so they're "saved," but it hasn't delivered the full life that it was supposed to, and so they're bitter. Deep down, they believe God has let them down. Which is often something they can't share with those around them, because they are the leaders who are supposed to have it all together. And so they quietly suffer, thinking this is the good news.

It is the gospel of the goats,
and it is lethal.

God is not a slave driver.
The good news is better than that.

This distinction,
the one between entrance and enjoyment,
has another serious implication,
one having to do with how we tell the story.
When you've experienced the resurrected Jesus, the mystery hidden in the fabric of creation, you can't help but talk about him. You've tapped into the joy that fills the entire universe, and so naturally you want others to meet this God. This is a God worth telling people about.

This is the problem with some Gods—you don't know if they're good, so why tell others a story that isn't working for you?

Witnessing, evangelizing, sharing your faith—when you realize that God has retold your story, you are free to passionately, urgently, compellingly tell the story because you've stepped into a whole new life and you're moved and inspired to share it. When your God is love, and you have experienced this love in flesh and blood, here and now, then you are free from guilt and fear and the terrifying, haunting, ominous voice that whispers over your shoulder, "You're not doing enough." The voice that insists God is, in the end, a slave driver.

Have nothing to do with that God.

We're invited to trust the retelling now,
so that we're already taking part in the kind of love that can overtake the whole world.

This leads us to another distinction,
one that takes us back to the recurring question,
What is God like?

Many have heard the gospel framed in terms of rescue. God has to punish sinners, because God is holy, but Jesus has paid the price for our sin, and so we can have eternal life. However true or untrue that is technically or theologically, what it can do is subtly teach people that Jesus rescues us from God.

Let's be very clear, then: we do not need to be rescued from God. God is the one who rescues us from death, sin, and destruction. God is the rescuer.

This is crucial for our peace, because we shape our God, and then our God shapes us.

Inquisitions, persecutions, trials, book burnings, blacklisting—when religious people become violent, it is because they have been shaped by their God, who is violent. We see this destructive shaping alive and well in the toxic, venomous nature of certain discussions and debates on the Internet. For some, the highest form of allegiance to their God is to attack, defame, and slander others who don't articulate matters of faith as they do.

We shape our God, and then our God shapes us.
A distorted understanding of God,
clung to with white knuckles and fierce determination,
can leave a person outside the party,
mad about a goat that was never gotten,
without the thriving life Jesus insists is right here,
all around us,
all the time.

Jesus was very clear that this destructive, violent understanding of God can easily be institutionalized—in churches, systems, and ideas. It's important that we're honest about this, because some churches are not life-giving places, draining people until there's very little life left. That God is angry, demanding, a slave driver, and so that God's religion becomes a system of sin management, constantly working and angling to avoid what surely must be the coming wrath that lurks behind every corner, thought, and sin.

**We shape our God,
and then our God shapes us.**

Our beliefs matter.
They matter now, for us,
and they matter then, for us.
They matter for others, now,
and they matter for others, then.

There is another dimension to the violent, demanding
God, the one people need Jesus to rescue them from.
We see it in the words of the older brother, when he says
he "never even disobeyed." You can sense the anxiety
in his defense, the paranoid awareness that he believed
his father was looking over his shoulder the whole time,
waiting and watching to catch him in disobedience. The
violent God creates profound worry in people. Tension.
Stress. This God is supposed to bring peace, that's
how the pitch goes, but in the end this God can easily
produce followers who are paralyzed and catatonic,
full of fear. Whatever you do, don't step out of line or
give this God any reason to be displeased, because who
knows what will be unleashed.

Jesus frees us from that,
because his kind of love simply does away with fear.
Once again, the words of the father in the story,
the one who joyously, generously declares:
"You are always with me,
and everything I have is yours."

There is another truth here,
beyond heaven and hell and anxiety and violence.
It is a truth at the heart of the gospel,
a truth both comforting and challenging,
both healing and unnerving.

Each brother has his own version of events,
his own telling of his story.
But their stories are distorted,
because they misunderstand the nature of their father—
we've seen that.
But there's another reason their stories aren't true,
a reason rooted less in the nature of God,
and more in the sons' beliefs about themselves.

The younger brother believes that he is cut off,
estranged, and no longer deserves to be his father's son,
because of all the terrible things he's done.

His badness is his problem, he thinks.

He's blown the money on meaningless living until he
was face down in the gutter, dragging the family name
through the mud in the process. He is convinced that his
destructive deeds have put him in such a bad state that
he doesn't even *deserve* to be called a son anymore.

Now, the older brother believes that the reason he
deserves to be a son is because of all of the good he's

done, all of the rules he's obeyed, all of the days he's "slaved" for his father.

His goodness is to his credit, he thinks.

The younger brother's wrongs have led him away from home, away from the family, deep into misery. This is true.

His sins have separated him from his father.

The second truth, one that is much more subtle and much more toxic as well, is that the older brother is separated from his father as well, even though he's stayed home.

His problem is his "goodness."
His rule-keeping and law-abiding confidence in his own works has actually served to distance him from his father.

What we learn in his speech to his father is that he has been operating under the assumption that his years of service and slaving were actually earning him good standing with his father.

He thinks his father loves him because of how obedient he's been.
He thinks he's deserving because of all the work he's done.
He thinks his father owes him.

Our badness can separate us from God's love,
that's clear.
But our goodness can separate us from God's love as
well.

Neither son understands that the father's love was never
about any of that. The father's love cannot be earned,
and it cannot be taken away.

It just is.

It's a party,
a celebration,
an occasion without beginning and without end.

It goes on,
well into the night,
and into the next day,
and the next
and the next.
Without any finish in sight.

Your deepest, darkest sins and your shameful secrets are
simply irrelevant when it comes to the counterintuitive,
ecstatic announcement of the gospel.

So are your goodness, your rightness, your church
attendance, and all of the wise, moral, mature decisions
you have made and actions you have taken.

It simply doesn't matter when it comes to the surprising,
unexpected declaration that God's love simply is yours.

There is nothing left for both sons to do but to trust.
As Paul writes in Philippians 3,
"Let us live up *to what we have already attained.*"

The father has taken care of everything.
It's all there,
ready,
waiting.
It's always been there,
ready,
waiting.

Our trusting,
our change of heart,
our believing God's version of our story
doesn't bring it into existence,
make it happen, or create it.

It simply is.

On the cross, Jesus says,
"Father, forgive them,
for they do not know what they are doing" (Luke 23).

Jesus forgives them all,
without their asking for it.

Done. Taken care of.

Before we could be good enough or right enough,
before we could even believe the right things.

Forgiveness is unilateral.
God isn't waiting for us to get it together,
to clean up, shape up, get up—
God has already done it.

As it's written in 2 Corinthians 5: "God was reconciling
the world to himself in Christ, not counting people's sins
against them."
In 2 Timothy 1 it says, "God . . . has saved us . . . not
because of anything we have done but because of his
own purpose and grace."
In Romans 5 we're told, "At just the right time, when we
were still powerless, Christ died for the ungodly."
And in Titus 3 it's written, "When the kindness and love
of God our Savior appeared, he saved us, not because
of the righteous things we had done, but because of his
mercy."

Not because of anything we've done.
When we were still powerless.
Because of his mercy.

We're saved in our death,
and in our life.

In our release of the ego,
and in our clinging to it.
In our smallness,
and in our bigness.

Jesus meets and redeems us in all the ways we have it together and in all the ways we don't, in all the times we proudly display for the world our goodness, greatness, and rightness, and in all of the ways we fall flat on our faces.

It's only when you lose your life that you can find it, Jesus says.

The only thing left to do is trust.
Everybody is already at the party.
Heaven and hell,
here,
now,
around us,
upon us,
within us.

———————

Whose version of her story will that woman handing me that piece of paper trust? All of the men who told her she was nothing, who hit her and abused her, who abandoned her and despised her? Or will she trust another story about herself, the one in which she is loved, valued, forgiven, pure, and beautiful?

If you were sitting with me
on that stage on a Sunday morning,
holding that piece of paper in your hand
she'd just handed you,
I know how you'd respond.
You'd tell her another story,
a better one.

Of course.
Now, turn that around.
Because we all have a bit of her in us,
we hand God our piece of paper.
And we listen,
while we're told a better story.
Because the good news is better than that.

CHAPTER 8

THE END IS HERE

And so we arrive at the last chapter. The end is here. We've explored a fairly vast expanse of topics, from heaven and hell to God, Jesus, joy, violence, and the good news that is better than that, among other things.

A story, then, to begin the ending.

One night when I was in elementary school, I said a prayer kneeling beside my bed in my room in the farmhouse we lived in on Dobie Road in Okemos, Michigan. With my parents on either side of me, I invited Jesus into my heart. I told God that I believed that I was a sinner and that Jesus came to save me and I wanted to be a Christian.

I still remember that prayer.
It did something to me.
Something *in* me.

In an innocent grade school kind of way, I believed that God loved me and that Jesus came to show me that love and that I was being invited to accept that love.

Now I am well aware of how shaped I was by my environment, how young and naive I was, and how easy it is to discount emotional religious experiences. With very little effort a person can deconstruct an experience like that by pointing out all of the other things going on in that prayer, like the desire to please one's parents and the power of religion to shape a child. But however helpful that may be, it can easily miss the one thing that can't be denied: What happened that night was real. It meant something significant then and it continues to have profound significance for me. That prayer was a defining moment in my life.

I tell you that story because I believe that the indestructible love of God is an unfolding, dynamic reality and that every single one of us is endlessly being invited to trust, accept, believe, embrace, and experience it. Whatever words you find helpful for describing this act of trust, Jesus invites us to say yes to this love of God, again and again and again.

As we experience this love, there is a temptation at times to become hostile to our earlier understandings, feeling embarrassed that we were so "simple" or "naive," or "brainwashed" or whatever terms arise when we haven't come to terms with our own story. These past understandings aren't to be denied or dismissed; they're to be embraced. Those experiences belong. Love demands that they belong. That's where we were at that point in our life and God met us there. Those moments were necessary for us to arrive here, at this place at this time, as we are. Love frees us to embrace all of our history, the history in which all things are being made new.

Our invitation, the one that is offered to us with each and every breath, is to trust that we are loved and that a new word has been spoken about us, a new story is being told about us.

Now, that word "trust," that is a rare, difficult word.

Cynicism we know, and skepticism we're familiar with. We know how to analyze and pick apart and point out inconsistencies. We're good at it. We've all been burned, promised any number of things only to be let down. And so over time we get our guard up, we don't easily believe anything and trust can become like a foreign tongue, a language we used to speak but now we find ourselves out of practice.

Jesus invites us to trust that the love we fear is too good to be true is actually good enough to be true. It's written in one of John's letters in the scriptures that "what we will be has not yet been made known." Jesus invites us to *become*, to be drawn into this love as it shapes us and forms us and takes over every square inch of our lives. Jesus calls us to repent, to have our minds and hearts transformed so that we see everything differently.

It will require a death,
a humbling,
a leaving behind of the old mind,
and at that same time it will require an opening up,
loosening our hold,
and letting go,
so that we can receive,
expand,
find,
hear,
see,
and enjoy.

This invitation to trust asks for nothing more than this moment, and yet it is infinitely urgent. Jesus told a number of stories about this urgency in which things did not turn out well for the people involved. One man buries the treasure he's been entrusted with instead of doing something with it and as a result he's "thrown outside into the darkness." Five foolish wedding attendants are unprepared for the late arrival of the groom and they end up turned away from the wedding with the chilling words "Truly I tell you, I don't know you." Goats are sent "away" to a different place than the sheep, tenants of a vineyard have it taken from them, and weeds that grew alongside wheat are eventually harvested and "tied in bundles to be burned."

These are strong, shocking images of judgment and separation in which people miss out on rewards and celebrations and opportunities. Jesus tells these stories to wake us up to the timeless truth that history moves forward, not backward or sideways. Time does not repeat itself. Neither does life. While we continually find grace waiting to pick us up off the ground after we have fallen, there are realities to our choices. While we may get other opportunities, we won't get the one right in front of us again. That specific moment will pass and we will not see it again. It comes, it's here, it goes, and then it's gone. Jesus reminds us in a number of ways that it is vitally important we take our choices here and now as seriously as we possibly can because they matter more than we can begin to imagine.

Whatever you've been told about the end—
the end of your life,
the end of time,
the end of the world—
Jesus passionately urges us to live like the end is here,
now,
today.

Love is what God is,
love is why Jesus came,

and love is why he continues to come,
year after year to person after person.

Love is why I've written this book, and
love is what I want to leave you with.

May you experience this vast,
expansive, infinite, indestructible love
that has been yours all along.
May you discover that this love is as wide
as the sky and as small as the cracks in
your heart no one else knows about.
And may you know,
deep in your bones,
that loves wins.

ACKNOWLEDGMENTS

A thousand thanks to:

Erwin McManus for the wise counsel in that Cuban
restaurant in Los Angeles in the summer of 2005

Jon Bell and Brian Mucci for insisting on the car ride
home from Chicago that now is the time

Rob Strong for twenty years of saying exactly what I
needed to hear

Jim Olsson for that conversation on the bus

Dr. Tandy Champion, Shane Hipps, Brad Gray, Mark Baas,
Don Golden, Matt Krick, Dr. Dave and Linda Livermore,
Lucy Russo, Gabor George Burt, and those I can't recall
at this time who read a draft along the way and gave
much needed perspective and feedback

Alex and Tom for listening to me read an early draft out loud

Zach Lind for saying "wrecking ball" under his breath several times in a row

all the Bell, Childress, and Olsson clans for their unflagging love and support, and especially to my parents, Rob and Helen, for suggesting when I was in high school that I read C. S. Lewis

My sister, Ruth Olsson, for the conversation about the painting

Chris Ferebee for keeping his cool for ten years

Mickey Maudlin for bringing the editor love, draft after draft after draft after draft

Mark Tauber, Claudia Boutote, Laina Adler, Michele Wetherbee, Mandy Chahal, Katy Renz, Lisa Zuniga, and all of the fine folks at HarperOne in San Francisco for believing in this book from day one

Mike Volkema for telling me that story about the chair

everybody at Mars Hill, how would I ever begin to thank you for all you've given me?

Kristen. Are you free Thursday night?

FURTHER READING

On Jesus In every square inch of creation, see Robert Farrar Capon's *The Mystery of Christ*

On hell, see C. S. Lewis's *The Great Divorce*

On the cross, see Mark Baker's *Proclaiming the Scandal of the Cross*

On the two sons in the story Jesus tells, see Timothy Keller's *The Prodigal God*

On growth and change and all that, see Richard Rohr's *The Naked Now* and *Everything Belongs*

On who and what God is, see Huston Smith's *The Soul of Christianity*

On resurrection and new creation, see N. T. Wright's book *Surprised by Hope*

For more on:

- getting people clean water, go to 20liters.org and charitywater.org

- justice and human rights, go to ijm.org

- nuclear weapons and the pressing need to have fewer of them, go to twofuturesproject.org

- microfinance and working for measurable change among the most oppressed and forgotten, go to worldrelief.org or call their global headquarters in Baltimore and ask to speak to Don Golden. He'll be thrilled.